North Carolina Legal Research

Carolina Academic Press
Legal Research Series

Tenielle Fordyce-Ruff, Series Editor
Suzanne E. Rowe, Series Editor Emerita

❧

Arizona, Third Edition—Tamara S. Herrera

Arkansas, Second Edition—Coleen M. Barger, Cheryl L. Reinhart & Cathy L. Underwood

California, Fourth Edition—Aimee Dudovitz, Sarah Laubach & Suzanne E. Rowe

Colorado, Second Edition—Robert Michael Linz

Connecticut—Jessica G. Hynes

Federal, Second Edition—Mary Garvey Algero, Spencer L. Simons, Suzanne E. Rowe, Scott Childs & Sarah E. Ricks

Florida, Fourth Edition—Barbara J. Busharis, Jennifer LaVia & Suzanne E. Rowe

Georgia—Nancy P. Johnson, Elizabeth G. Adelman & Nancy J. Adams

Idaho, Third Edition—Tenielle Fordyce-Ruff

Illinois, Second Edition—Mark E. Wojcik

Iowa, Second Edition—John D. Edwards, Karen L. Wallace & Melissa H. Weresh

Kansas—Joseph A. Custer & Christopher L. Steadham

Kentucky, Second Edition—William A. Hilyerd, Kurt X. Metzmeier & David J. Ensign

Louisiana, Third Edition—Mary Garvey Algero

Massachusetts, Second Edition—E. Joan Blum & Shaun B. Spencer

Michigan, Third Edition—Cristina D. Lockwood & Pamela Lysaght

Minnesota—Suzanne Thorpe

Mississippi—Kristy L. Gilliland

Missouri, Third Edition—Wanda M. Temm & Julie M. Cheslik

New York, Third Edition—Elizabeth G. Adelman, Theodora Belniak, Courtney L. Selby & Brian Detweiler

North Carolina, Third Edition— Brenda D. Gibson, Julie L. Kimbrough, Laura P. Graham & Nichelle J. Perry

North Dakota—Anne E. Mullins & Tammy R. Pettinato

Ohio, Second Edition—Sara Sampson, Katherine L. Hall & Carolyn Broering-Jacobs

Oklahoma—Darin K. Fox, Darla W. Jackson & Courtney L. Selby

Oregon, Fourth Edition, Revised Printing—Suzanne E. Rowe & Megan Austin

Pennsylvania, Second Edition—Barbara J. Busharis, Catherine M. Dunn, Bonny L. Tavares & Carla P. Wale

Tennessee, Second Edition—Scott Childs, Sibyl Marshall & Carol McCrehan Parker

Texas, Second Edition—Spencer L. Simons

Washington, Second Edition—Julie Heintz-Cho, Tom Cobb & Mary A. Hotchkiss

West Virginia, Second Edition—Hollee Schwartz Temple

Wisconsin—Patricia Cervenka & Leslie Behroozi

Wyoming, Second Edition—Debora A. Person & Tawnya K. Plumb

❧

North Carolina Legal Research

Third Edition

Brenda D. Gibson

Julie L. Kimbrough

Laura P. Graham

Nichelle J. Perry

Tenielle Fordyce-Ruff, Series Editor
Suzanne E. Rowe, Series Editor Emerita

Carolina Academic Press

Durham, North Carolina

Library of Congress Cataloging-in-Publication Data

Names: Gibson, Brenda D., author. | Kimbrough, Julie L., author. | Graham, Laura P., author. | Perry, Nichelle J., author.
Title: North Carolina legal research / by Brenda D. Gibson, Julie L. Kimbrough, Laura P. Graham, Nichelle J. Perry.
Description: Third edition. | Durham, North Carolina : Carolina Academic Press, LLC, [2019] | Series: Legal Research Series | Includes bibliographical references and index.
Identifiers: LCCN 2019018868 | ISBN 9781531013400 (alk. paper)
Subjects: LCSH: Legal research--North Carolina.
Classification: LCC KFN7475 .C48 2019 | DDC 340.072/0756--dc23
LC record available at https://lccn.loc.gov/2019018868

eISBN 978-1-5310-1341-7

Carolina Academic Press

700 Kent Street
Durham, North Carolina 27701
Telephone (919) 489-7486
Fax (919) 493-5668
www.cap-press.com

Printed in the United States of America.

Summary of Contents

Contents

List of Tables and Figures

Tables

Figures

Series Note

The Legal Research Series published by Carolina Academic Press includes titles from many states around the country as well as a separate text on federal legal research. The goal of each book is to provide law students, practitioners, paralegals, college students, laypeople, and librarians with the essential elements of legal research in each jurisdiction. Unlike more bibliographic texts, the Legal Research Series books seek to explain concisely both the sources of legal research and the process for conducting legal research effectively.

Acknowledgments

This edition of *North Carolina Legal Research* continues to fill the unique niche of providing "a North Carolina-focused, process-based legal research textbook for law students and lawyers." We have tried to stay true to the goal of the first two editions: to help North Carolina students, attorneys, and lay persons become savvy researchers.

In addition to updating the substantive information that appeared in the second edition, we have changed the tone of the book a bit, in the hope that it will be more inviting and more accessible to current law students. We have also added an Introduction that explains the important role research plays in helping lawyers achieve their ultimate goal of constructing reliable answers to legal questions. Finally, we have heavily emphasized how to research using electronic and low-cost sources of legal information, in keeping with the trend in the legal academy and the profession.

This edition follows the established footprint of the prior editions, but we have expanded the book's discussion of foundational sources of law within each chapter. We have combined the chapters on constitutions and statutes, and we have placed the information about North Carolina citation rules in its own chapter rather than in an appendix.

Special thanks to Suzanne Rowe for her vision and leadership in creating this state-specific research series and for providing us with the tremendous opportunity to work on a new edition of *North Carolina Legal Research*. We are also grateful to Tenielle Fordyce-Ruff, series editor, for approving our four-member "dream team" and for lending us her keen eyes and superb editorial skills; her input has made this a much better book than it would have otherwise been. And we are grateful to Scott Childs and Sara Sampson, authors of the second edition, whose work provided us with a great foundation to build upon.

All four of us have our own supporters, without whom we would not have reached the finish line of this project.

From Brenda Gibson: "Special thanks to my husband, Adolph Simmons, Jr., and my children, Drayton and Andrew, who gave me the space and encouragement to complete this project; and to my NCCU School of Law colleagues and my legal writing colleagues nationwide who supported me and cheered me to the finish line."

From Julie Kimbrough: "Special thanks to Douglas B. Hill for his constant support and encouragement of this project; to UNC Law Library Director Anne Klinefelter for her excellent advice and her vision for scholarship; and to all my talented colleagues at the UNC Law Library for their support and inspiration."

From Nichelle Perry: "Special thanks to my husband, Alexander, for his support; to my sons, Jordan and Ian, for reminding me of what is important; to NCCU Law Library Assistant Director Austin Martin Williams for manning the ship when I needed to write; and to the staff of the NCCU Law Library for their support."

From Laura Graham: "Thank you to my husband, Joseph, and my daughter, Ellen, for keeping me company in the late hours when I was hard at work on this book; to my colleagues in the Legal Analysis, Writing, and Research Program at Wake Forest University School of Law, including our wonderful law librarians; and especially to Sally Irvin, my research partner extraordinaire for the last twenty years, who has taught me almost everything I know about legal research."

Introduction

Answers to Preliminary Questions to Get You Started

I. What Is Legal Research?

As lawyers, the essence of our work is constructing answers to legal questions. And just as carpenters have toolboxes filled with various tools they use on their different projects, lawyers must have toolboxes filled with various tools to help them construct answers to legal questions.

The question might be simple (like building a bookshelf): What are the elements of first-degree burglary in North Carolina? The question might be a little more complex (like building a backyard shed): How have North Carolina courts defined the various elements of first-degree burglary in cases similar to my client's case? Or the question might be quite difficult and multi-faceted (like building a house): What arguments can I make to convince the court that this North Carolina statute is unconstitutional?

Legal research is one of the tools that all lawyers need in their toolboxes in order to construct answers to legal questions. Legal research refers to the process lawyers (and law students) use to find and evaluate authorities that are relevant to particular legal questions. The authorities a lawyer discovers through that process provide the legal rules that apply to a particular issue. The authorities can also provide information about what those rules mean and perhaps even how those rules have been applied to similar legal questions.

II. Why Is Legal Research an Important Skill?

Many veteran lawyers argue that legal research is the most important tool lawyers can have in their toolboxes. In a recent survey conducted by LexisNexis,

86% of the senior attorneys who responded considered legal research skills highly important in young associates. Additionally, 81% considered advanced legal research skills highly important, and an even higher percentage, 88%, considered proficiency in using paid research services highly important.[1]

Moreover, studies show that most young associates spend between 40% and 60% of their time conducting legal research.[2] Perhaps this is one reason why the American Bar Association, in Standard 302(b), explicitly recognizes the importance of legal research, listing it as one of the skills in which law schools must demonstrate they are training students to be competent.[3]

III. What Makes Legal Research Challenging?

Legal research can be extremely interesting and even fun; lawyers take great satisfaction in finding the best authorities to answer a legal question or support a legal argument. But legal research can also be difficult, especially for new legal researchers, for several reasons.

First, legal research requires great *intellectual effort.* You cannot formulate an effective research strategy or develop effective search terms unless you understand the contours of the legal question you need to answer. Thus, before you jump headfirst into your research, you must spend some time "getting your bearings." You must become familiar with the facts that give rise to the legal question. You may need to spend some time familiarizing yourself with the area(s) of law the question touches on. You must orient yourself to the specific end goal of your research process: Will you simply be reporting your research findings? Will you be using your findings to craft a legal document such as a memorandum or brief? Are you constrained to the authorities from a particular jurisdiction, or should your research be broader? Asking these questions early will help you stay focused and be efficient in your research process.

You must also be knowledgeable about the various sources of authority that are available and how those sources relate to each other. Acquiring this knowledge can take a long time, and new legal researchers may find the maze of different sources of authority confusing. Is this authority primary or secondary?

---

1. LexisNexis, *Hiring Partners Reveal New Attorney Readiness for Real World Practice* 3 (2015), lexisnexis.com/documents/pdf/20150325064926_large.pdf.

2. *Id.*

3. ABA Standard 302(b), *available at* americanbar.org/content/dam/aba/publications/misc/legal_education/Standards/2018-2019ABAStandardsforApprovalofLawSchools/2018-2019-aba-standards-chapter3.pdf.

Is it mandatory or persuasive? Is it promulgated by a court, or a legislature, or an agency? What if you find two authorities that conflict with each other? What if the only authority you can find that is relevant to your question is not from your jurisdiction?

And you must discipline yourself to pause periodically in your research process to evaluate what you are finding. Today's law students are good *finders,* having grown up in the Google age. And being able to find authorities quickly is a good thing. But legal research is about much more than *finding* authorities. It requires you to constantly ask yourself certain questions about the authorities you are finding. Are they in fact relevant to the question you need to answer? Are they reliable? Do they contain references to other helpful authorities that you should consult? The process of legal research is intertwined with the process of legal analysis, and you will often find yourself toggling back and forth between finding and evaluating.

Second, legal research is *messy.* It is not a linear process. You cannot complete a legal research task simply by consulting a master checklist and moving through the steps in an orderly fashion. Yes, there are strategies for effective legal research that are tried and true, and this book explains those strategies. But how you use those strategies may differ widely from one legal question to the next.

Moreover, even after you have found and evaluated the relevant authorities and have moved on to drafting a document that conveys your analysis of the legal question, you may discover that you need to return to the research process. Perhaps in your analysis you have discovered a new angle to the question—a new issue—and you need additional authority to help you address it. Perhaps you have realized that the authority you thought was helpful on a particular point is not really "on point." Or perhaps you simply need more authority to support your analysis of a particular issue.

Third, legal research is an *ongoing effort.* The law is not static, and it is important to know (1) how to verify that the authorities you are using to answer your legal question are still "good" and (2) how to update your research in the course of a particular project.

Finally, legal research can be *costly.* And because legal employers and clients value *efficiency* in the research process, you must not only know what sources to consult; you must also be strategic about the cost-effectiveness of your research. Legal authority can be found through sophisticated online research on expensive commercial platforms, and sometimes that is the most cost-effective way to go about your research. Legal authority can be found through a number of free online resources, and sometimes that is the most cost-effective way to go about your research. Legal authority can still be found in print, and sometimes that is the most cost-effective way to go about your research. Sometimes the process requires you to use a combination of these resources. A wise lawyer always thinks about the most cost-effective and time-saving approach to the task before she begins researching.

IV. Why Is This Book Useful?

Recognizing the importance of legal research and the challenges it presents (especially for novices), this book undertakes to give law students and attorneys in North Carolina as well as other jurisdictions a set of research tools to add to their toolboxes. Much of the content of this book applies to all legal research, regardless of the jurisdiction; whether you are researching a federal issue, an issue of North Carolina law, or an issue of some other state's law, the strategies for developing a research plan and for engaging in the process of legal research are very similar.

However, each jurisdiction has certain unique structures and sources of legal authority, resulting in nuances that may affect the planning and execution of legal research in that jurisdiction. This book focuses on the structures and sources of legal authority in North Carolina.

Because questions of North Carolina law may sometimes overlap with questions of federal law, portions of this book do contain some discussion of the federal legal system and sources of federal authority. However, those portions are meant to supplement the book's coverage of legal research in North Carolina, and this book does not exhaustively cover federal legal research. This book also contains some references to the legal systems and sources of law of other states; those references are mainly intended to highlight key differences between conducting legal research in North Carolina and conducting legal research in other states.

V. How Is This Book Organized?

Chapter 1 provides an overview of the categories of legal authority you will encounter in your legal research, whether in North Carolina or another jurisdiction. It also discusses the various sources of legal authority within North Carolina, focusing on the three branches of North Carolina's government. Chapter 2 describes the research process generally, then provides specific strategies for planning an efficient, effective research process. Chapter 3 explores the various secondary sources available to North Carolina researchers. Chapters 4 through 8 cover the key legal authorities needed to research constitutions and statutes, legislative history, administrative materials, and cases, respectively.

Chapter 9 covers the key sources of court rules and rules of ethics and professional conduct that govern the practice of law in North Carolina. Chapter 10 covers the basic citation rules adopted by North Carolina and points to some resources that are useful in constructing correct citations to North Carolina authorities. Finally, the book contains several appendices intended to direct readers to additional resources relevant to legal research in North Carolina.

Because efficient research often involves using both print and online resources, we have included information about both kinds of resources in each chapter. For some kinds of legal sources, we cover how to research them online first; for others, we cover how to research them in print first. This is a deliberate choice on our part; for each source, we have chosen to describe the research methods in the order that makes the most sense for that particular source.

Our hope is that this book will become an invaluable tool in the toolboxes of law students and lawyers interested in North Carolina legal research.

North Carolina Legal Research

Chapter One

Foundations of Legal Research and Analysis

The nuances and complexities of the law make it both exciting and challenging. This is also true of legal research. To fully appreciate these complexities, a legal researcher must first have basic knowledge about the structure of the law and our legal system. You will not be able to use the various tools in your toolbox effectively to research the law without understanding what the law is.

I. Review of the Law and the American Legal System

The word *law* may refer to a single statute or rule, a body of rules, or an entire legal system. In the United States, rules of law originate chiefly from two sources. One source is *enacted law*, which includes constitutions, statutes, regulations, and ordinances promulgated by bodies at the highest level of government (the United States Congress, for example) and at many lower levels (including city or town councils and local boards). Chapters 4 and 6, respectively, describe how to research constitutions, statutory law, and administrative law. The other source is *case law*, which is derived from judicial opinions issued by both federal and state courts. Chapters 7 and 8 describe how to research case law.

A. Constitutions and Statutory Law

Constitutions set out the fundamental principles of law governing a country or state. They are broad, overarching documents that create each branch of government and outline its powers and duties. Our United States Constitution, adopted by Congress in 1787, is the supreme law of the land, but it is limited in scope to those powers specifically vested in, and not prohibited to be exercised by, the federal government.[1] In 1789, North Carolina became the twelfth state to ratify the United States Constitution. North Carolina also has its own state constitution; the current version is the third iteration and was adopted in 1971.[2]

In the federal government and in most state governments, including North Carolina, legislators are empowered by the citizens to make laws to address existing problems, prevent future problems, and improve the citizenry's lives. Both the United States Congress and the North Carolina General Assembly[3] are bicameral bodies composed of a Senate and a House of Representatives. Our federal Congress and state General Assembly members attempt to reach consensus by debating, compromising, voting, and enacting laws, commonly referred to as *statutes*. Most statutes are framed very broadly and are generally applicable to the citizenry. Thus, the term *statutory law* refers to the broad-based laws enacted by federal and state lawmakers.

1. The Federal System

Statutes enacted by the United States Congress are known as *public laws*.[4] These laws apply to everyone in the country and typically address issues of national importance, such as taxes, drug safety, crime, banking, and national defense. See Appendix A describing how a bill is enacted into law in the U.S. Congress.

2. North Carolina

In North Carolina, a bill is enacted into law in two steps (with a few exceptions). First, the bill must be ratified by both chambers of the North Carolina

---

1. The Tenth Amendment of the Constitution defines the relationship between the federal government and the governments of the fifty states. All rights not prescribed to the federal government or prohibited in the federal constitution to be exercised by the federal government were reserved to the states.

2. The first North Carolina Constitution was drafted and adopted by the fifth provincial congress in December, 1776. After significant amendments were made to that constitution in 1835, and another constitutional convention was held in 1862–63 to add other amendments, including secession from the Union, a second state constitution was adopted in 1868. The third and current state constitution was adopted in 1971.

3. Note that state legislatures have a variety of official names, depending on the state.

4. Congress occasionally enacts private laws, which apply only to persons named in the laws. These laws do not appear in the United States Code. Instead, they are published as slip laws and collected in the *Statutes at Large*.

General Assembly. Ratification requires both chambers to pass identical legislation that has been separately proposed and discussed in both chambers. Second, after ratification, most bills must be signed by the Governor before becoming law. Regardless of which chamber a bill begins in, after ratification and signature of the Governor, the bill becomes a session law. See Appendix B detailing how a bill is enacted into law in the North Carolina General Assembly.

B. Judicial Opinions

Both the federal and state court systems are hierarchical; the weight of a court's authority depends on its position within the court system of the relevant jurisdiction. There are typically three levels in both the federal and state court systems: (1) the trial court; (2) the intermediate appellate court; and (3) the highest appellate court.

Trial courts are where most cases are initiated and adjudicated. However, as we discuss in the North Carolina-specific materials below, often, administrative cases or minor cases, such as traffic violations, estate matters, or small claims matters, are initiated and adjudicated before the cases reach the trial court level. Additionally, there are specialized trial courts in the federal and state court systems, such as the federal Tax Court, which resolves tax cases, and the North Carolina Business Court, which addresses complex business litigation. In some jurisdictions, there may also be other specialized trial courts that are subject-matter specific, e.g., family court (addressing family law only) or drug court (addressing drug-related offenses only).

Most litigation is concluded at the trial court level;[5] however, trial court decisions usually do not have precedential value because of the trial courts' low

---

5. More than 2,200 appeals and petitions were filed in the North Carolina Court of Appeals during FY 2017–18, compared to approximately 655 appeals and petitions for review filed in the North Carolina Supreme Court during that same period. 2017–2018 NCAOC Ann. Rep. N.C. Jud. Branch 11–12, nccourts.gov/assets/documents/publications/2017-18_North_Carolina_Judicial_Branch_Annual_Report.pdf. There were more than 4,600 appeals filed in the United States Court of Appeals for the Fourth Circuit (which has jurisdiction over North Carolina federal appeals) during FY 2017–2018, FY 2017–2018 Admin. Off. U.S. Cts. Federal Ct. Mgmt. Stat. 1, uscourts.gov/sites/default/files/data_tables/fcms_na_appsumary0930.2018.pdf, compared to approximately 6,300 filings in the United States Supreme Court (though only 69 of those cases were argued) during that same period. C.J. John Roberts, 2018 Year-End Rep. Fed. Judiciary, Appendix Workload, 12, supremecourt.gov/publicinfo/year-end/2018year-endreport.pdf.

position in the hierarchy of courts. In fact, in many states, including North Carolina, trial court decisions are not published, and in many cases, no written opinion is produced.[6] Under the concept of *stare decisis*[7] in case law, a lower court must adhere to the legal rules set forth by higher courts within the same jurisdiction in cases involving the same issues. Thus, trial court decisions have very little, if any, precedential value. Accordingly, when researching North Carolina state case law, your focus will be on appellate cases.

1. Federal Courts

a. Generally

Federal trial courts are called the United States District Courts. There are ninety-four districts in the United States. Some states, such as South Carolina, have only one federal district, while other states have several districts. North Carolina has three districts—the Western District, the Middle District, and the Eastern District.

The federal intermediate appellate courts are called the United States Courts of Appeals. There are thirteen federal Circuits, each with a Court of Appeals. Eleven of those Circuits are composed of groups of geographically close states. For example, North Carolina is in the Fourth Circuit, which also includes South Carolina, Virginia, West Virginia, and Maryland. The United States Court of Appeals for the District of Columbia, located in Washington, D.C., is a Circuit of its own, as is the United States Court of Appeals for the Federal Circuit, established in 1982. Unlike the other Courts of Appeals, which have broad jurisdiction over claims arising under federal law, the Federal Circuit has appellate jurisdiction over only certain limited subjects, such as patent appeals.

The highest appellate court in the federal court system is the Supreme Court of the United States, which hears appeals from any of the thirteen federal Courts of Appeals and other specialized appellate courts. Most of the appeals heard by the Supreme Court are based upon discretionary review. The Supreme Court may also hear limited appeals from state supreme courts if those appeals involve issues of federal law. See Appendix C, Geographic Boundaries of the

---

6. North Carolina trial courts do not issue written opinions.

7. *Stare decisis* is a Latin phrase meaning "to stand by things decided." Black's Law Dictionary explains that in the legal context, *stare decisis* represents the doctrine of precedent requiring courts to follow earlier judicial decisions of a higher court when the same points of law are addressed. *Stare decisis*, *Black's Law Dictionary* 1626 (10th ed. 2014).

United States Judicial System, for a map of the federal judicial system's geographic boundaries.

Table 1-1. Federal Court System

U.S. District Courts (trial level)

U.S. Courts of Appeals (intermediate appellate level)

U.S. Supreme Court (highest appellate level)

b. Routes of Appeal

In North Carolina, a litigant with a federal law claim typically files the action in the appropriate United States District Court sitting within the state—the Western District, the Middle District, or the Eastern District. An appeal from the trial court's decision would be heard in the United States Court of Appeals for the Fourth Circuit. And an appeal from the Fourth Circuit's decision would be heard in the Supreme Court of the United States, if the Supreme Court agrees to hear the appeal.

2. North Carolina Courts

a. Generally

In North Carolina, there are two divisions of the trial court: the District Court and the Superior Court. Administrative matters, small claims, family law cases, and some misdemeanor criminal cases are resolved in District Court. The Superior Court, which is divided into eight divisions and fifty districts across the state's 100 counties, hears all felony criminal cases, civil cases involving more than $25,000, and misdemeanor and infraction appeals from District Court. As in most states, North Carolina trial courts do not typically publish their decisions, and their decisions do not have precedential value.

Table 1-2. The North Carolina Court System

N.C. District and Superior Courts (trial level)

N.C. Court of Appeals (intermediate appellate level)

N.C. Supreme Court (highest appellate level)

b. Routes of Appeal

A litigant who is dissatisfied with the result in District or Superior Court may appeal to the North Carolina Court of Appeals. Fifteen Court of Appeals judges sit in rotating panels of three to hear appeals from lower courts. One of the few exceptions to this rule is appeals in death penalty cases, which bypass the Court of Appeals and go directly to the North Carolina Supreme Court. At the Court of Appeals level and above, the focus of the court's review is on errors of law or errors in judicial interpretation in the lower courts. Appellate courts do not make determinations of fact, but rather rely on the factual findings made by the lower courts.

The highest appellate court in North Carolina is the North Carolina Supreme Court. The Supreme Court is composed of a Chief Justice and six Associate Justices who hear cases as a single panel (usually referred to as *en banc*). As provided by state statute, the Supreme Court may accept some cases on appeal in its discretion.[8] Generally, however, the Court hears appeals of right.[9] See Figure 7.1, North Carolina Courts System Routes of Appeal, *infra*, showing how a case works its way through the North Carolina court system.

3. Courts of Other States

With a few minor differences, most other states' judicial systems share the same three-tiered structure as North Carolina. Some states may split their intermediate appellate courts into a civil and criminal branch, or may have a number of appellate courts, or may not have an intermediate appellate court at all. Additionally, a few states call their highest appellate court something other than "supreme court." However, there are more similarities among states

---

8. N.C. Gen. Stat. § 7A-31 (2017) allows the Supreme Court to hear discretionary cases through the issuance of a writ for discretionary review.

9. N.C. Gen. Stat. § 7A-27 et seq. (2019) provides appeals of right to the Supreme Court, including first degree murder cases leading to a death sentence, termination of parental rights cases, certain mandatory complex business cases from the Business Court, class action certifications under N.C.R. Civ. P. 23, and rate making cases from the Utilities Commission. Appeals of right to the Supreme Court also lie (1) from decisions of the Court of Appeals that involve substantial questions arising under the state or federal Constitution; (2) from cases in which one member of a three-judge panel of the Court of Appeals dissents from the majority opinion; and (3) from cases the Court of Appeals heard en banc, when the time for filing a motion for rehearing has passed or a motion for rehearing has been denied. N.C. Gen. Stat. § 7A-30 (2017).

than differences, making it relatively easy for a legal researcher to toggle among any number of jurisdictions if necessary.

C. Executive and Administrative Law

The executive branch of the government is headed by the President of the United States at the federal level and by the Governor at the state level. At both the federal and state levels, the executive branch includes administrative agencies that are responsible for administering and enforcing statutes.

1. Federal

a. President

The President of the United States has the authority to enter into *treaties* with other countries (with the advice and consent of the Senate). Additionally, the President has the authority to issue *executive orders* to regulate administrative agencies and government officials. These treaties and executive orders are law.

b. Administrative Agencies

Federal administrative agencies promulgate *rules* and *regulations*. These agencies also hear cases involving disputes over agency rules and alleged violations of those rules; this process produces *agency decisions*, which are much like court decisions. These agency rules and regulations and agency decisions are law. Examples of federal administrative agencies include the Food and Drug Administration (FDA), which regulates the nutrition labels on the food you buy; the Federal Aviation Administration (FAA), which creates airline safety regulations; and the Environmental Protection Agency (EPA), which regulates the environment.

2. North Carolina

a. Governor

In most states, including North Carolina, the Governor is the highest officer of the state's executive branch. Like the President of the United States, the Governor carries out the duties prescribed to the office by the state constitution and statutes. Those duties include creating documents that may become law, such as state budget provisions. In North Carolina, the Governor has the authority to issue executive orders, just like the President of the United States.

b. Administrative Agencies

Like federal administrative agencies, state administrative agencies administer and enforce the law, creating rules and regulations and hearing disputes involving agency rules and alleged violations of those rules. These agency rules and regulations and agency decisions are also law. Examples of North Carolina administrative agencies include the Building Code Council, which regulates construction methods; the North Carolina Medical Board, which prohibits unlicensed physicians from practicing in the state; and the Secretary of State's office, which oversees many of the economic and business-related operations of the state government.

II. Types of Authority

Now that we have reviewed the sources of our law and the structure of our legal systems, it is time to discuss the very important concept of *weight of authority*. As noted in the Introduction and more fully discussed in Chapter 2, Developing a Research Strategy, one of the primary tasks of a legal researcher is finding the most authoritative sources to help answer the legal question.

The most authoritative sources will come from a person or entity authorized by the jurisdiction's constitution to say what the law is. As discussed above, in addition to the constitution, there is statutory law created by legislatures and case law created by courts. There may also be administrative rules or decisions from the executive branch. Preferably, the answer to a legal researcher's question will be found in one of these sources from the governing jurisdiction. However, there are other types of legal authority that may also be helpful in different ways, even if they do not have the force of law and even if they are from another jurisdiction.

A. Primary Authority and Secondary Authority

Primary authority is law issued by bodies constitutionally authorized to pronounce the law, i.e., the legislative, executive, and judicial branches of the government. Within each jurisdiction, that jurisdiction's constitution is the supreme law. The legislature enacts statutes requiring or prohibiting certain actions. The agencies within the executive branch interpret and enforce those statutes by making detailed rules and regulations regarding exactly how they must be implemented. Judges hear arguments when legal disputes arise and issue opinions settling those disputes. All of these institutions produce primary authority within their specific jurisdiction.

Unlike primary authority, *secondary authority* is not the law itself. Instead, secondary authority explains or comments on the law and is typically written by those who teach (law professors), practice (attorneys), or otherwise dabble in the law (editors and publishers of legal publications). Secondary authority serves as an important tool for finding and understanding primary authority, as Chapter 3 discusses.

B. Mandatory vs. Persuasive Authority

Primary authority from the jurisdiction where a legal issue arises is called *mandatory authority*. It is *mandatory* because it is the law that must be applied by courts within that jurisdiction in cases that involve the same legal question. Another term for *mandatory authority* is *binding authority*. For example, a case decided by the North Carolina Supreme Court on a particular legal issue is *mandatory* or *binding* on North Carolina trial courts and on the North Carolina Court of Appeals when they hear cases involving that same legal issue.

The term *persuasive authority* refers to (1) primary authority from a jurisdiction other than the one in which a particular case is being heard and (2) all secondary authority, regardless of the source. Researchers typically search first for mandatory primary authority, although persuasive primary authority can often be useful in developing an analysis or argument, especially when there is no mandatory primary authority on your legal question.

See Table 1-3, illustrating examples of mandatory and persuasive authority and their position in the hierarchy of authority.

Table 1-3. Examples of Authority in North Carolina Legal Research

	Mandatory Authority	Persuasive Authority
Primary Authority	North Carolina Constitution	Virginia Constitution
	North Carolina General Statutes	South Carolina Code of Laws
	North Carolina Supreme Court and Court of Appeals Decisions	Georgia Supreme Court and Court of Appeals Decisions
Secondary Authority		Treatises
	—	Law Review articles
		Legal encyclopedias

III. Tools for the Toolbox

1. The law comes from all levels of government—federal, state, and local—and from all three branches within those levels—legislative, executive, and judicial.
2. There is a hierarchy in government and in the sources of law that determines which sources a legal researcher will ultimately utilize.
3. Primary authority is usually best, and it is mandatory when applied to a legal issue that arises in the same jurisdiction where the primary authority was created.
4. Secondary authority is never mandatory, but it can be extremely useful in finding and understanding primary authority.

Chapter Two

The Research Process: Strategies and Techniques

I. Overview of the Research Process

Google has become our go-to source for everything, and legal research is not exempt from this phenomenon. Unfortunately, many people, even lawyers, start their legal research with a broad Google search. While Google may be helpful in searching for the best restaurants or directions to the mall, it is not an effective way to begin your legal research. Google will not provide you with a clear path to the authority that controls the legal issue you are researching. With Google, you must often wade through a massive number of responses, most of which have little or no relation to the issue you are researching. Put simply, Google should rarely be the first tool you reach for to begin constructing the answer to your legal question.

Even if you begin your research on one of the widely used electronic legal research platforms, you should remember that other formats (i.e., print) may be better for certain types of research. Do not assume that all laws are online, that all online laws are available in an easily searchable format, or that online laws are always up-to-date. A thorough legal researcher will utilize various formats for the most efficient research process.

The ultimate goal of legal research is to locate mandatory primary authority; to do so, you must be knowledgeable about effective legal research strategies. While legal research is not a linear process, legal professionals generally follow a series of steps designed to lead them to the most helpful authorities in a systematic way. Table 2-1 below provides an overview of the common steps in the legal research process and the order in which researchers often move through those steps.

As you become more proficient at legal research, you will learn how to adapt the process to fit the various research tasks you undertake; in other words, you will learn to be flexible in your approach to each legal research problem. For example, you might have enough background knowledge about the issue to allow you to skip Step 2, Consulting Secondary Sources, and move straight to looking for primary authority. However, for novice legal researchers, the following steps outline a tried and true process that will guide you to the best answers to the legal questions you are researching.

Table 2-1. Overview of the Legal Research Process

1. **Analyze.** Review the research problem to identify the issue, determine the jurisdiction, and develop search terms.
2. **Consult Background Sources/Secondary Sources.** Consult secondary sources that provide commentary, such as treatises, law review articles, and legal encyclopedias, to get context and background on your issue.
3. **Locate Primary Authority.** Look for primary authority such as constitutional provisions, statutes, administrative laws, and cases.
4. **Evaluate.** Evaluate and expand your research based on research leads from primary authorities.
5. **Update with Citators.** Use a citator service such as Shepard's or KeyCite to ensure your research is up to date.
6. **Stop Researching.** In general, your research is complete when you are satisfied that your research has led you to the most helpful authorities on your legal question and you begin to see the same authorities in your searches.

II. Preparing to Research and Getting Started

A. Analyzing Issues and Generating Search Terms

The key to successful research is gathering as much information as possible about the matter that you are researching, as early in the process as possible. You must gain a clear understanding of the subject of your research. Additionally, you must understand the parameters of your research project, including time limits, goals for the research, deadlines, and available research sources. For law students, this requires carefully reviewing the assignment and speaking with your professor to ensure that you understand the nature of the assignment. For practicing attorneys, this may require interviewing the client, reviewing preliminary court documents, and talking with colleagues. One of the most important questions you must address during this early stage is which jurisdiction's law controls your question. By identifying the controlling jurisdiction at an early stage of the project, you can more easily identify the sources that you will need to use in your research.

After identifying the parameters of your research and the controlling jurisdiction, you should begin brainstorming about search terms. Whether you are using print research materials or an online research platform, you often cannot use those resources effectively until you first identify the keywords or phrases that describe the legal question you are researching. Although search terms are generally legal terms, they may be common words that describe your research question. These words are often referred to as *search terms, keywords, research terms,* or *descriptive words.*

One way to develop these terms is to categorize the information presented by the facts.[1] This requires looking at: the *parties* involved, in terms of their legal status or relationship to each other; the *places*, in terms of both geography and the nature of the locations; *things*, both tangible and intangible; the *potential claims and defenses* that could be raised; and the *relief sought* by the complaining party.

Consider the following example. A wife divorced her husband several years ago. Due to the evidence regarding his lifestyle and his criminal past, the court found that under the totality of the circumstances, it was in the child's best interest to grant the mother custody and award only limited visitation to the father. The father has made significant changes in his life and now approaches you, his attorney, asking whether he would be successful in gaining joint custody of his child if he were to seek a modification of the existing custody order.

Table 2-2 provides examples of research terms you might use to begin researching this question based on the "categories" approach.

Table 2-2. Generating Research Terms

PARTIES: husband, wife, mother, father, child, spouse, family

PLACES: trial court, family court

THINGS: custody order, modification

POTENTIAL CLAIMS AND DEFENSES: child custody modification, motion for modification, child custody order

RELIEF: modification, new custody order

1. Amy E. Sloan, *Basic Legal Research: Tools and Strategies* 27-28 (7th ed. 2018).

B. Consulting Secondary Sources

After developing your initial research terms, you should begin using secondary sources, such as treatises, law review and journal articles, and legal encyclopedias, to get context and background on your issue. Secondary sources provide commentary on the law written by legal professionals or legal publishers. They are useful for locating primary authority because they provide citations to and summaries of statutes, administrative laws, and cases. However, remember that secondary sources are not the law. Secondary sources are covered further in Chapter 3.

C. Locating Primary Authority

Although secondary sources can be an excellent way to find primary authority, you should always search directly for primary authority—constitutional provisions, statutes, administrative rules and regulations, and cases—via the conventional search methods discussed in this book. The secondary sources you consult may not reference all the primary authorities directly related to your research question.

D. Evaluating the Authorities

After locating primary authorities (or better yet, even as you are locating them), you must evaluate everything you have found to determine its relevance to and its impact on your research question. This is one of the most important aspects of legal research—assessing the results of your research to determine how the authorities help you answer your legal question.

E. Updating

Finally, you must ensure that the authorities you have found represent the current law. Law is a living, growing body of knowledge that is constantly changing. In the practice of law, therefore, access to the most current information is critically important for four reasons. First, and most importantly, a lawyer must know if the authority she is relying on is still "good law." For a case, determining whether it is still good law means finding out whether the case has been reversed on appeal to a higher court or overruled by a subsequently decided case in the same jurisdiction. For a statute or administrative rule, determining whether it is still good law means verifying that it has not been amended, repealed, or superseded by subsequent legislation or struck down by a case.

Second, in addition to confirming that your authorities are still good law, you need to know how the authorities have been treated by subsequent sources. While law found online or in print through a comprehensive, modern research process will likely still be good law, the law changes quickly, and updating your research is still critically important. Law is being created, decided, and applied daily. Even if your authorities have not been directly affected, subsequent developments might strengthen or weaken their application in certain situations.

Third, updating your authorities is a good way to find cases similar to yours. This can be an especially useful research tool if, for example, you have found little or no mandatory case law and are having difficulty identifying additional cases. The process of updating usually identifies any related authorities that have been issued after your case was decided.

Fourth, updating ensures you have found the most current information from each source. Some online platforms are currently updated by the organization supporting the database. For some print sources, initial updating may involve searching books, pocket parts, and pamphlets in combination. Regardless of the source, be sure to determine how current the information is that you are using by looking at scope notes (for databases) and date references or copyright dates (for print information). Then, after locating the most current information from each source throughout your research process, you should also use a *citator* to complete the updating process.

Citators are used to determine how an authority has been treated by later actions of a court, legislature, or agency. A citator will tell you whether subsequent authorities still follow the authorities you have located or whether your authorities have been reversed, overruled, or criticized by later courts. Many refer to the process of updating as *Shepardizing* because the first major tool for updating was *Shepard's Citations.*[2] Now, however, there are two other well-known citators: *KeyCite,* available on Westlaw, and *BCite,* available on Bloomberg. Information on updating with citators will be provided in later chapters as appropriate.

2. Shepard's Citations Service was the preeminent name in citators for over 100 years. Although it bears a trademarked name, its ubiquitous existence as the only citator for generations of attorneys and researchers across the country led to the creation of the term "Shepardizing" to describe the act of updating the law with a citator.

F. Stopping Your Research

Deciding when to stop researching is often very difficult. As a new researcher, you may feel that you should not stop searching until you find the perfect primary authority that directly answers your research question. However, most often, that perfect authority does not exist, and it would be inefficient to continue searching for it indefinitely. With experience, you will learn when to stop; generally, the time to stop is when your research process leads you the same primary authorities over and over.

III. Choosing Sources of Legal Information

A. Introduction

Before electronic research platforms transformed the world of legal research, access to legal information generally required a visit to a law library. Print copies of primary and secondary legal sources sat in practical obscurity on library shelves, and serious researchers had no choice but to become very familiar with complex, specialized legal publications and how to use them. Locating relevant case law required access to print case reporters and digests. Print legal treatises provided in-depth analysis of legal topics and pointed researchers to relevant statutes and cases. Copies of legislation, regulations, and government reports were distributed in paper to selected libraries around the country as part of the Federal Depository Library Program (FDLP).[3] For many years, academic law libraries in North Carolina received print copies of briefs filed with the North Carolina Supreme Court and the North Carolina Court of Appeals. Thus, libraries essentially had a monopoly on access to the law itself as well as to the sources that provided explanation and commentary to help researchers understand the law.

In the age of the Internet, libraries no longer play the role of gatekeeper, and researchers with access to a computer and an Internet connection can find the law in seconds using a simple keyword search. Case law is freely accessible and searchable on Google Scholar. The federal government and all fifty states

3. Additionally, the Printing Act of 1895 created the Federal Depository Library Program ("FDLP"). Copies of many published laws and documents from all three branches of government are widely available through more than 1,200 public libraries that participate in the FDLP.

provide free online access to statutes and legislation. Cornell University's Legal Information Institute (LII) website[4] provides full-text access to federal statutes, regulations, and Supreme Court decisions; LII has also created a free legal dictionary and encyclopedia, with legal experts contributing the content. Historical legal sources are being digitized by libraries and publishers at a rapid rate.[5]

As a new legal researcher, you may feel overwhelmed by the massive amount of information available to you. In law school classes like Contracts and Torts, you read judicial opinions as a tool to help develop the skill of legal analysis. By the time you graduate from law school, you will have read thousands of cases, and you will have learned how to examine a fact pattern and identify the legal rules that apply. Legal research and writing skills provide the bridge between your doctrinal classes and the daily reality of law practice. It is important to practice navigating through research platforms and to become familiar with the structure of the legal information sources offered there. Developing effective legal research skills requires time, repetition, and focus on the structure and organization of the law. As an attorney, you will use the skills of legal research, legal analysis, and legal writing together on a daily basis. To do so effectively, you must become very familiar with your options for accessing legal information in all formats, and you must learn to become an efficient researcher in order to save your clients time and money.

B. Fee-Based Sources of Legal Information

As a law student, you have unlimited access to one or more of the three major commercial legal platforms: Westlaw, Lexis, and Bloomberg. Westlaw, a subsidiary of Thomson Reuters, and Lexis, a subsidiary of Elsevier, are the best known commercial legal research service providers in the United States and around the world. These vast electronic platforms are the culmination of years of print legal publishing. Bloomberg is a more recent entrant into the commercial legal database market, having acquired the legal publisher Bureau of National Affairs (BNA) in 2011. These sophisticated platforms contain billions of pages of content and are the result of massive corporate investment in technology and algorithms, a computer process that allows users to enter a keyword search to find relevant results. Making an effort to become familiar

4. law.cornell.edu.

5. HeinOnline (home.heinonline.org) and Gale's Making of Modern Law (gale.com/primary-sources/making-of-modern-law) include large collections of digitized primary and secondary legal sources.

with Westlaw, Lexis, and Bloomberg while in law school can offer significant benefits for future real-world legal research tasks.

For many attorneys, these services are part of their daily research routine. Large law firms spend hundreds of thousands or even millions of dollars annually on Westlaw, Lexis, and Bloomberg subscriptions.[6] Many law firms have an exclusive contract with either Westlaw or Lexis, so it is important to practice using both platforms during law school, even if you prefer one platform over the other. If you work in a small firm, solo practice, or government setting, you may have access to only one of the big three platforms, and your content may be limited to your state's primary legal sources and local or regional secondary materials. And in some settings, you may not have access to these services at all. Whether and to what extent you use them in practice will depend on your employer's and your clients' financial resources.

Fortunately, there are low-cost alternatives to Westlaw, Lexis, and Bloomberg. Two leading low-cost research providers are Fastcase and Casemaker. As a member of your state bar association, you will generally have free or low-cost access to either Fastcase or Casemaker.[7] The North Carolina Bar Association currently provides its members (including student members) with free access to Fastcase.

In the last decade, Fastcase and Casemaker have disrupted the traditional Westlaw/Lexis model for commercial legal platforms, and legal researchers now benefit from access to databases that have similar features, including keyword searching, access to primary legal materials, and tools for citation analysis.[8] While these low-cost platforms have many similar features to the major commercial platforms, they offer limited secondary source content, because the vast majority of secondary legal materials were originally published in print by companies now owned by Westlaw, Lexis, or Bloomberg. Thus, for example, *Nimmer on Copyright* is available electronically only on Lexis, and *Wiggins Wills and Administration of Estates in North Carolina* is available electronically only on Westlaw. Additional information about the coverage of the various online platform is included in future chapters. See Table 2-3 for a list of leading fee-based, online legal information providers.

---

6. ALM Intelligence Survey of Law Firm Management, Library, and Research Professionals, 2017.

7. fastcase.com/coverage/; casemakerlegal.com.

8. fastcase.com/about/; public.casemakerlegal.net/products/casemaker/.

Table 2-3. Fee-Based Sources Providing Legal Information

Bloomberg	bloomberglaw.com
Casemaker	casemaker.us.com
Fastcase	fastcase.com
Lexis	LexisAdvance.com
Westlaw	westlaw.com

C. Free Legal Information Sources

In the United States, free federal and state legal information is widely available online from both official and unofficial sources. The legislative, executive, and judicial branches of government are the official sources of laws, and those entities may publish legal information directly or through a commercial publisher in print and online formats. Commercial publishers also publish unofficial versions of primary legal sources; in many cases, the unofficial versions are the most commonly used and up-to-date sources available. The distinction between official and unofficial sources can be critical in legal research, particularly if the source is cited in a document submitted to a court. As we will discuss in Chapter 9, Court Rules and Other Practice Rules, attorneys filing documents with a court must be aware of the source of the legal information they are viewing online and must follow the court's rules for citing those legal sources.

The United States government produces massive amounts of official legal information and research products. For most of the country's history, public access to legal information sources has depended on decisions made by individual government entities and statutory requirements that either help or hinder free public access. With the establishment of the United States Government Printing Office (GPO) in 1861, the United States took a major step toward ending a long history of privately printed laws and government information.[9] Fortunately for legal researchers, the vast majority of this information is now available at no cost online on the GPO Website, Govinfo.gov.[10] GPO

9. In 2014, the Government Printing Office became the Government Publishing Office, and we use the latter term throughout the rest of this book."

10. *See* govinfo.gov/.

has also made great strides toward authenticating its electronic versions of federal laws using a digital signature.[11]

In North Carolina, free primary legal information from all three branches of state government is readily available online. The North Carolina General Assembly Website provides access to current legislation, session laws, and the North Carolina General Statutes. Opinions of the North Carolina Court of Appeals and Supreme Court from 1998 to the present are available online through the North Carolina Courts website. The North Carolina Office of Administrative Hearings provides an online version of the *North Carolina Register* and *North Carolina Administrative Code.* Chapter 6 will discuss the sources of North Carolina administrative law in more detail. See Table 2-4 for North Carolina government websites that provide free access to primary law sources.

Table 2-4. Government Websites for North Carolina Primary Law Sources

North Carolina Constitution	
	ncleg.gov/Legislation/constitution/ncconstitution.html
North Carolina Statutes	
	ncleg.gov/gascripts/statutes/Statutes.asp
North Carolina Cases	
	appellate.nccourts.org/opinions/
North Carolina Administrative Law	
	oah.state.nc.us

IV. Basic Strategies for Using Legal Information

Technology has revolutionized our daily lives, and it has forever changed the way that research is conducted. When you first encounter Westlaw, Lexis, and Bloomberg, it may seem like an impossible task to locate relevant legal information among thousands of search results and a multitude of unfamiliar primary and secondary legal information sources. While you might conduct your legal research exclusively online, there are some important reasons to understand how print legal resources are constructed. If you have the opportunity to spend some time using legal materials in print, you will quickly notice sim-

11. *See* govinfo.gov/about/authentication.

ilarities in the way legal sources are organized. American legal sources have a structure and organization that is distinctive, and it is this structure that provides the foundation for the major commercial electronic legal platforms.

A. Print Research Techniques

Generally, primary legal sources are first published chronologically. Court opinions appear online and in print in the order the opinions are handed down by the courts. Legislation approved by Congress or a state legislature receives a number that reflects the order in which that legislation was passed. Not surprisingly, legal publishers became extremely popular by providing subject-based access to primary legal sources. Annotated codes recompile statutes in a subject arrangement that allows researchers to start with a major legal topic and narrow their search to the specific legal issue at hand. For American case law, the West Digest System and Topic and Key Number System provides the framework for print research and analysis of judicial opinions.

One of the easiest ways to search in print sources is to start with a known item: either the name of or the citation to a primary or secondary legal source. Print sets of statutes generally include an index volume containing the popular names of legislative acts. West Digests include a volume that provides alphabetical listings of cases by party name. Legal citations generally consist of three parts: the volume number of the source, the abbreviation of the title of the source, and the page or section number where the item is located. Chapter 10 discusses legal citations in greater detail.

Browsing is one of the most reliable ways to locate information in print legal sources. Virtually all law books contain a *table of contents* at the beginning of each volume indicating the structure and content of the information found there. The table of contents is an excellent choice for researchers wishing to see relevant topics that relate to their legal issue. The companion to the table of contents is the *index*, generally found at the end of a single volume or set of statutes or a treatise. The index is a detailed, alphabetical list of terms (search terms) that are located in the document or source. An index usually includes cross-references and related terms that help researchers with a critical step in the research process: connecting their own search terms to the specific legal terms used by a primary legal source.

B. Online Research Techniques

Westlaw and Lexis continue to offer the traditional print-based table of contents and index structure in their online statutes. In fact, many users find online statutes easier to browse than the print versions because online annotations contain hyperlinks that allow researchers to immediately review relevant sources. Westlaw also continues to provide the Digest and Key Number System in online form.

C. Using Annotated Resources

The major legal publishers built their businesses by hiring lawyers and subject experts to create editorial content that explains primary law, makes connections between relevant primary and secondary sources, and provides citation analysis and updating tools. Almost all of the features available in commercial print legal sources have been replicated in the electronic databases created by these publishers.

One of the most important research tools, both in print and online, is *annotations.* Annotations are short blurbs, created by editors, that accompany statutory provisions and provide references to related case law, regulations, legislative history, and relevant secondary sources. As Chapter 4 explains more fully, annotated codes can be an excellent place to start your research if there is a statute that is relevant to your legal question. Annotations are abundant in both primary and secondary legal sources. *American Law Reports* (A.L.R.) is a secondary source containing longer topical annotations (brief articles) that include references to federal and state case law, statutes, and secondary sources. A.L.R. is discussed in more detail in Chapter 3.

D. Using Citators and Case Analysis Tools

Another significant benefit of access to fee-based legal platforms is their citators. Citators for case law are discussed in greater detail in Chapter 8. Westlaw, Lexis, and Bloomberg offer online citators (KeyCite, Shepard's, and BCite, respectively) which are tools that allow users to enter a legal citation for a case, statute, regulation, or administrative decision to find out whether that source is still good law. Citators are a popular updating tool for legal researchers and an excellent starting point for those who already know of a relevant case, statute, or regulation. As we will discuss throughout this book, your legal research is complete only when you have ensured that your primary authorities are still valid law in your jurisdiction.

V. Final Notes on the Research Process

For new legal researchers, following the process outlined in Table 2-1 is an excellent way to ensure that your research is organized and focused on the relevant legal sources. For more seasoned researchers, familiarity with the primary and secondary legal sources in your area of practice will allow you to be flexible in your approach to the research process. Effective legal research builds on the foundation of information-gathering and analysis of the relevant facts and legal issues. As your research moves forward, it is important to track your progress through well-organized notes or research logs so that you will avoid duplicating your earlier research. Structured notes will also allow you to easily narrow or expand on your earlier research when new information on your legal issue arises. Throughout this book, you will find strategies for improving research efficiency, identifying connections between sources of legal information, and making legal information sources work for you.

VI. Tools for the Toolbox

1. Develop and follow a research process.
2. Determine what format(s) you will use to perform your research.
3. Update, Update, Update.
4. Document your research.

Chapter Three

Secondary Sources

I. Introduction

When you are researching a legal question, your ultimate goal is to locate mandatory primary authorities (statutes, regulations, cases) that address that question. However, in some circumstances, you might find it easier to locate and understand those primary authorities if you begin your research process by consulting *secondary sources*. Secondary sources are indispensable tools in a researcher's toolbox.

The term *secondary sources* encompasses a wide variety of authorities that contain commentary about the law; this commentary is considered secondary to the law itself. Secondary sources are written by law professors, legal experts, the editorial staff of legal publishing companies, and many other legal professionals and legal organizations. Although some secondary sources are highly regarded and carry significant weight, secondary sources are never mandatory authority in any jurisdiction. However, secondary sources can be extremely valuable to a legal researcher in several ways.

First, secondary sources can provide helpful background information when you are researching an area of the law you are unfamiliar with. For example, if you are working on a case that involves a complicated tax question, and you are not well-versed in tax law, you might benefit from consulting a secondary source that explains tax law broadly and provides context for your specific legal question. Having that context will make it easier for you to generate good search terms that will lead you to primary authorities, and it will help you understand those primary authorities when you begin to read them.

Next, secondary sources often contain references to primary authorities, saving you time in your research process. Some states have jurisdiction-specific secondary sources; for example, North Carolina researchers can consult *Strong's North Carolina Index* (discussed more fully later in this chapter), a legal encyclopedia that both explains the law and provides citations to primary authorities that are mandatory for North Carolina courts.

Third, secondary sources can be a useful tool when you are researching an area of the law that is new or not well-developed. For some legal questions, there simply is not much primary authority to work with; in these instances, the commentary in secondary authorities becomes critical to your ability to analyze the legal question.

Finally, secondary sources can help you sift through the authorities you find, especially if you have found a large quantity of relevant primary authorities. Today's law students and young lawyers are excellent *finders*, but a wise legal researcher will pause periodically in her research process to evaluate the usefulness of what she has found thus far. Secondary sources can aid you in this evaluation, perhaps by helping you narrow your focus (so that you can weed out authorities that initially appear helpful but turn out not to be) or broaden your focus (so that you can find additional relevant primary authorities in places you did not think to look before). Thus, although the basic legal research process introduced in Chapter 2 appears to be linear, you may need to consult secondary sources at various points in your research process.

A few caveats about secondary sources are in order at this point. First, a good researcher will carefully assess the quality and credibility of a given secondary source before relying on it either as a research tool or as persuasive authority for a legal analysis or argument. Secondary sources come in all shapes and sizes, and they are not equally reliable or equally weighty. Second, a good legal writer will avoid citing secondary authority in a memo, brief, or other legal document unless there is no (or very little) primary authority available to support a proposition. Finally, if you use secondary sources to locate primary authority, do not cite the primary authority without first reading it for yourself. The secondary source might misstate the law or omit key information, or it might reference primary authority that is no longer valid (for example, a statute that has been repealed or a case that has been overruled). Secondary authorities are wonderful tools for finding primary authority, but they are not substitutes for it.

A. Secondary Sources and Practice Materials

Legal encyclopedias, legal treatises, legal periodicals (law reviews and journals), *American Law Reports* Annotations, and Restatements of the Law are the five "traditional" secondary sources of law. Each of these sources provides a unique view of the law and may serve different purposes throughout your research process. These five secondary sources will be addressed in depth in this chapter. Table 3-7, at the end of this chapter, summarizes the strengths and weaknesses of these five sources.

Many other secondary sources of law might be categorized as practice materials. These include recent materials from continuing legal education programs (CLEs), legal forms (e.g., examples of motions and complaints), pattern jury instructions, uniform laws, and law-related blogs. Practice materials are covered briefly at the end of this chapter.

B. Selecting the Most Relevant Secondary Source

Secondary sources have different strengths and weaknesses and can be used in different ways while you are researching. If you understand these strengths and weaknesses, you will be able to select the most useful secondary authorities for your research project. Researchers are typically working under time constraints and do not have time to review an extensive array of secondary materials. Rather, a wise researcher will spend some focused time consulting one or two carefully selected secondary sources at the outset, thereby saving valuable time and gaining the necessary background knowledge to continue the research process. Table 3-1 below outlines the key steps in selecting appropriate secondary sources for a research project.

Table 3-1. Outline for Selecting Appropriate Secondary Sources for a Research Project

1. Determine what you are trying to accomplish with your research. Are you searching for a quick, broad overview of a legal topic or a deep but narrowly focused description of a discrete area of law? Do you need criticism and analysis of existing law? Do you need recommendations for changes in the law?
2. Examine the chart in Table 3-7 explaining the strengths and weaknesses of the five traditional secondary sources.
3. Match the purposes of your research with one or two secondary sources that have strengths relevant to your research purposes. For example, if you need a broad, descriptive overview of a legal topic, a legal encyclopedia would likely be a better secondary source to consult than a Restatement. If you need detailed analysis of a narrow topic, with citations to primary authority, an *American Law Reports* Annotation would likely be a better secondary source to consult than a treatise.

C. Print versus Online

When researching in secondary sources, many researchers find that being able to quickly browse and view related content is important because it provides the context in which to understand information efficiently. Some researchers consider print sources superior to online sources in providing this context. However, online vendors have steadily improved the presentation of secondary sources by including browsable tables of contents and other helpful features typically found in print.

As you will see in the remainder of this chapter, not all secondary sources are available online, and of those that are, some can be accessed only for a fee. Likewise, many law libraries have pared down their print resources to cut costs, and secondary authorities have been a fertile area for elimination. Thus, on any given research project, you may need to consult both print and online sources to find relevant secondary authority.

In general, whether you are researching in print or online, you will use a similar three-step process for most secondary sources. First, locate the relevant material in the main text, using the index, a keyword search, or table of contents. Second, read the relevant material, taking notes on what you learn about your research question and what research leads you find. Third, update what you have found to make sure you are relying on the most current information for each source.

II. Legal Encyclopedias

Legal encyclopedias are among the most commonly consulted secondary sources. Like other kinds of encyclopedias you may have used, legal encyclopedias provide a general overview of the law on a variety of topics. Most legal encyclopedias are multi-volume publications that organize information alphabetically by topic. Although it is uncommon to cite legal encyclopedias in legal documents, they can be very good sources of background information on a topic; they often help you focus your research and guide you to primary authorities as well as other relevant secondary authorities.

Some states have state-specific legal encyclopedias. These vary in their content and level of detail. In North Carolina, *Strong's North Carolina Index* functions as an encyclopedia, although it may be slightly less descriptive than other states' legal encyclopedias. There are also two main national legal encyclopedias, *American Jurisprudence, Second Series* (Am. Jur. 2d) and *Corpus Juris Secundum* (C.J.S.).

A. *Strong's North Carolina Index*

Strong's North Carolina Index is a 30-plus-volume encyclopedic treatment of North Carolina law, currently in its fourth edition. When researching a North Carolina question of law, *Strong's*, rather than Am. Jur. 2d or C.J.S., is often the best starting point.

Like most legal encyclopedias, *Strong's* describes the law generally, without commentary, and provides citations to North Carolina cases as well as citations to relevant provisions of the North Carolina Constitution, the North Carolina General Statutes, court rules, and sometimes law review and journal articles. Because it is a West publication, *Strong's* also provides references to relevant West Topics and Key Numbers, making it a useful tool for finding related authorities from other jurisdictions. For more about the West Topic and Key Number System, see Chapter 8.

The two most helpful features of the print version of *Strong's* are the Index and the Words and Phrases Index, the latter of which contains an alphabetical list of specific words and phrases that have been judicially defined and citations to the cases where the definitions appear. Typically, both indexes are located at the end of the main volumes. In either index, you can locate the relevant sections of *Strong's* using key search terms. *Strong's* also provides a Table of Cases; if you have a case name, you can use this Table to find a discussion of that case in *Strong's*. Each volume of *Strong's* is updated with an annual cumulative pocket part, and the set is also updated with quarterly cumulative supplements.

Strong's is also available on Westlaw. You can find it by entering "Strong's North Carolina Index" in the universal search bar or via the North Carolina Secondary Sources database. You can browse the *Strong's* database using a table of contents approach, or you can search the full text by using keywords to generate search terms, as described in Chapter 2. The *Strong's* database also incorporates the contents of the separately published "archived" edition. The *Strong's* database is updated at least quarterly.

B. American Jurisprudence, 2d

Am. Jur. 2d is an "A to Z text statement of American laws, both state and federal."[1] Its A to Z coverage includes both civil and criminal law topics and

1. https://1.next.westlaw.com/Browse/Home/SecondarySources/TextsTreatises/AmericanJurisprudence2d?transitionType=SearchItem&contextData=%28sc.Default%29# (see Scope Note).

Figure 3-1. Excerpt from *Strong's North Carolina Index*

For Educational Use Only

20 N.C. Index 4th Landlord and Tenant § 107

Strong's North Carolina Index 4th | October 2018 Update

Landlord and Tenant
Keith A. Braswell, J.D., of the staff of the
National Legal Research Group, Inc. and Elizabeth M. Bosek, J.D.

VI. Residential Tenant Security Deposits

§ 107. Limitation on amount of tenant security deposit

Topic Summary | Correlation Table | References
West's Key Number Digest
- West's Key Number Digest, Landlord and Tenant K 1401

National Background
As to security deposits, generally, see Am. Jur. 2d, Landlord and Tenant §§ 105 to 109.

Statutes:

A security deposit in a residential tenancy may not exceed two weeks' rent if the tenancy is week to week, one and one half months' rent if the tenancy is month to month, or two months' rent for terms greater than month to month.[1]

Cases:

Requiring a security deposit of $150 from a mobile home tenant was not unlawful, although the rent had been $66, where the deposit was to be submitted in connection with new leases under which the monthly rental would be $145, and thus within the statutory maximum, regardless of whether the tenancy was month-to-month or year-to-year.[2]

Footnotes

1 N.C. Gen. Stat. Ann. § 42-51(b).

2 Cla-Mar Management v. Harris, 76 N.C. App. 300, 332 S.E.2d 495 (1985).

Source: Westlaw. Printed with permission of Thomson Reuters

both procedural and substantive law topics. The encyclopedia is maintained and updated by an editorial staff. Because Am. Jur. 2d is published by West, it provides references to the West Topic and Key Number System for each topic, allowing you to enter into the West Digest to find relevant primary authority on your topic.

Am. Jur. 2d has traditionally excelled at covering federal law issues, although it does cover state law as well. Thus, while you may occasionally find a reference in Am. Jur. 2d to some North Carolina authority on your research topic, it might not be the most efficient place to begin when researching a question of North Carolina law.

As with many comprehensive encyclopedias, researching in the print version of Am. Jur. 2d is best approached using the annually published multi-volume index, a set of separate softcover volumes usually located at the end of the main volumes. Using key words, you can search the index to locate relevant topic(s) and section number(s) in the main volumes. Each volume of the encyclopedia is updated with an annual cumulative supplement (pocket part) that includes relevant developments occurring after the publication of the latest bound volume.

Am. Jur. 2d is available on Westlaw; you can simply enter "Am. Jur." in the universal search bar, or you can access it via the Secondary Sources database. Westlaw updates Am. Jur. 2d quarterly. Am. Jur. 2d is also available on Lexis via the Secondary Materials database.

In both Westlaw and Lexis, using key words to search the encyclopedia's full text often retrieves many irrelevant passages. A nifty feature of the databases on both Westlaw and Lexis is the ability to browse Am. Jur. 2d's entire table of contents. You can browse the titles and use them as a menu by "drilling down"—continuing to select relevant topic and subtopic headings until you reach the encyclopedia text that addresses your research question.

C. *Corpus Juris Secundum*

Corpus Juris Secundum (C.J.S.), like Am. Jur. 2d, is a multi-volume legal encyclopedia that attempts to comprehensively cover American law, including all state and federal legal topics. Like Am. Jur. 2d, C.J.S. is published by West and contains references to the West Topic and Key Number System. One distinct feature of C.J.S. is the inclusion of "black letter" summaries of general rules of law throughout the text. Unlike Am. Jur. 2d, C.J.S. has traditionally been noted for its coverage of state law and its exhaustive citations to cases.

As with Am. Jur. 2d, the annually published multi-volume index for C.J.S. is the best place to begin researching in the print version of the encyclopedia. Each volume is updated with an annual cumulative supplement (pocket part).

C.J.S. is available as a database on Westlaw; simply enter "C.J.S." in the universal search bar or locate it from the Secondary Sources database. The table of contents feature is available for C.J.S., and you can search the full text using key words or natural language. C.J.S. is not available on Lexis.

III. Hornbooks, Professional Treatises, and Nutshells

The term "treatises" comprises a wide variety of books about specific areas of law. A treatise may be broadly focused, providing an excellent overview of a topic; or it may be narrowly focused, providing in-depth analysis. Treatises generally contain all or some of the following: (1) a review of how the law on the topic has developed; (2) an explanation of the legal rules on the topic; (3) an analysis of key statutes and cases on the topic; (4) a discussion of policy questions on the topic; and (5) citations to primary and secondary authority on the topic. A treatise exists for nearly every legal subject. The value of the information in any given treatise depends upon the reputation and knowledge of the author(s). You would probably not cite a treatise in a legal document, unless the treatise is very highly regarded and there is no primary authority you can cite instead.

A. Hornbooks

Hornbooks are one-volume treatises that are usually very detailed in their description and explanation of an area of law. Hornbooks are usually national in scope, and they usually cover the enduring principles of an area of law in some detail. They often include a limited number of citations to important statutes or seminal cases from select jurisdictions in the United States. Hornbooks are usually authored by law professors. Examples include *Hazen's Hornbook on the Law of Securities Regulation* and *Calamari & Perillo's Hornbook on Contracts*, both now in a sixth edition, and *Dobbs Hornbook on the Law of Torts*, formerly by Prosser and Keaton.

The *Understanding* series, originally published by Lexis and now published by Carolina Academic Press, and the *Mastering* series, published by Carolina Academic Press, both provide a broad overview of many legal subjects with limited citations to legal authority and therefore serve much the same purpose as hornbooks.

B. Professional Treatises

Professional treatises or "practitioner treatise series" are typically published in multi-volume sets; they usually provide much more detail than hornbooks, and they often contain extensive footnotes with citations to primary authorities. Because professional treatises often delve beyond enduring legal principles to describe the more rapidly developing areas of the law, they may be updated more often. Some authors of hornbooks also publish more detailed professional treatise versions. Examples of professional treatises include *Wright & Kane on Federal Courts*, *Nimmer on Copyright*, *Chisum on Patents*, and *Scott & Ascher on Trusts*.

There are several treatises that focus on North Carolina law. These treatises are extremely valuable when you are researching a North Carolina question; they are written by legal experts, they describe the law in North Carolina in detail, and they cite North Carolina primary authority, including cases, statutes, and regulations. Table 3-2 is a non-exhaustive list of North Carolina treatises.

Table 3-2. North Carolina Treatises

Brandis & Broun on North Carolina Evidence, 7th ed.
Lee's North Carolina Family Law, 5th ed. by Reynolds
North Carolina Civil Procedure, 3d ed. by Wilson
North Carolina Law of Torts, 3d ed. by Daye & Morris
North Carolina Torts, 2d ed. by Logan & Logan
North Carolina Trial Practice by Anderson
Robinson on North Carolina Corporation Law, 7th ed.
Webster's Real Estate Law in North Carolina, 6th ed.
Wiggins Wills and Administration of Estates in North Carolina, revised 4th ed.

C. Nutshells

West publishes a series of practical treatises geared toward law students, called the *Nutshell* series. There are hundreds of *Nutshells*, such as *Contracts in a Nutshell* and *Criminal Law in a Nutshell. Nutshells* typically provide very few, if any, citations to primary authority. Rather, they provide a broad overview of the main principles of law governing the legal topic and the context for understanding those principles. *Nutshells* are usually authored by law professors who are respected for their knowledge and expertise in particular legal subjects. *Nutshells* are national in scope and rarely provide specific information about the law of North Carolina. There are also several *Nutshells* covering areas of special interest to law students, such as *Law School Competitions in a Nutshell*, *Introduction to the Study and Practice of Law in a Nutshell*, and *Legal Drafting in a Nutshell.*[2] *Nutshells* are available online via a West Academic Study Skills

2. A full list of the titles in the *Nutshell* series is available at home.westacademic.com/nutshells.

Subscription Package. Many law schools purchase school-wide subscriptions for their students.

D. Finding Hornbooks and Treatises

Although using hornbooks and treatises is relatively easy, finding them can be challenging. A seasoned researcher may know the names of the hornbooks and treatises relevant to her field of research; however, for novice researchers, and for those who are researching an unfamiliar area, locating relevant hornbooks and treatises may be difficult. The most sensible approach is to ask someone who regularly researches or practices in the area. For example, in law school, ask a reference librarian or a faculty member. In a law firm, a librarian or an associate who researches in that area would be a good choice. You also might browse a library collection or use an online catalog in a larger library.

Because hornbooks and treatises are based upon the authors' hard-earned knowledge, and because a great deal of work is involved in the preparation and development of hornbooks and treatises, they are rarely available for free on the Internet. Because of their value, however, some hornbooks and treatises are available online for a fee through services such as Westlaw, Lexis, and Bloomberg. Browsing the secondary sources databases of these online services should lead you to the individual databases for these hornbooks and treatises, even if you do not know the titles.

Once located, either in print or online, hornbooks and treatises are usually best approached using the index or table of contents to find the information needed. Many of the hornbooks and treatises that are available online include a browsable table of contents.

IV. Legal Periodicals

The category of legal periodicals encompasses many different publications. The predominant sub-category of legal periodicals is law reviews and journals published by law schools. Almost all of the 203 ABA-approved law schools publish at least one law review or journal, and many publish two or more. Law students at these institutions select and edit the articles for publication. Some of the law reviews and journals publish articles on diverse subjects, while others focus on particular areas of the law, such as banking law or the First Amendment.

Typically, the featured articles are written by law professors or knowledgeable practitioners and are heavily footnoted. The articles may describe the law; but perhaps more importantly, they analyze, compare, and critique the law. The authors sometimes recommend changes in the law. Law student editors also occasionally write articles, usually referred to as notes or comments. When articles are focused on a relevant topic in your jurisdiction, the footnoted primary authorities may provide extremely important research information that can save hours of independent work.

The six law schools in North Carolina produce a number of law reviews and journals. Some of these publications specifically address North Carolina law, and some do not. Some are subject-specific. Law reviews and journals from the state's law schools are often excellent secondary sources for relevant legal analysis and critique. Law reviews and journals published by schools in other states may also contain useful articles as well, such as articles comparing North Carolina law to the law of other states. Table 3-3 sets out the law reviews and journals published by the six law schools in North Carolina.

Table 3-3. Law Reviews and Journals Published by Law Schools in North Carolina

Campbell University School of Law

- *Campbell Law Review*
- *Campbell Law Observer*

Duke University School of Law

- *Alaska Law Review* (published under the sponsorship of the Alaska Bar Association)
- *Duke Environmental Law & Policy Forum*
- *Duke Journal of Comparative & International Law*
- *Duke Journal of Constitutional Law & Public Policy*
- *Duke Journal of Gender Law & Policy*
- *Duke Law & Technology Review*
- *Duke Law Journal*
- *Duke Law Journal of Law & Contemporary Problems*

Elon Law School

- *Elon Law Review*

North Carolina Central University School of Law

- *North Carolina Central Law Review*
- *North Carolina Central Science & Intellectual Property Law Review*
- *North Carolina Central Environmental Law Review*

University of North Carolina School of Law

- *North Carolina Law Review*
- *North Carolina Banking Institute Journal*
- *North Carolina Journal of International Law*

- *North Carolina Journal of Law & Technology*
- *First Amendment Law Review*

Wake Forest University School of Law

- *Wake Forest Journal of Business & Intellectual Property Law*
- *Wake Forest Journal of Law & Policy*
- *Wake Forest Law Review*

If you already have a citation to a specific article (perhaps obtained via another secondary source), you can retrieve the article using that citation in Westlaw, Lexis, Bloomberg, and HeinOnline (described below). If not, you will need to use an index to locate citations to relevant articles.

A. Finding Law Review and Journal Articles Using the Index Method

Law review and journal articles are published in serial fashion and thus are not organized by subject. Moreover, individual law reviews and journals do not have their own indexes. There are two commonly used comprehensive print indexes for legal periodicals: the *Index to Legal Periodicals* and the *Legal Resources Index*. However, these print indexes require a lot of shelf space, they are cumbersome and time consuming to use, they are expensive to maintain, and there are now better alternatives. Thus, most law firms and libraries have eliminated print indexes. If you need to use a print index, seek the assistance of a law librarian.

Among the most common subscription-based online indexes of law review and journal articles are *LegalTrac*, which provides indexing from hundreds of law journals and legal publications since 1980, and an online version of the *Index to Legal Periodicals* (ILP), which indexes articles from legal journals, bar publications, and book reviews. ILP is available in several versions. The standard ILP product includes articles published since 1982. A separate database named *Index to Legal Periodicals Retrospective* covers articles published between 1908 and 1981. A combined product, named *Index to Legal Periodicals & Books: Current & Retrospective*, includes articles published between 1908 and the present. Many libraries subscribe to either *LegalTrac* or a version of ILP; these indexes are usually accessed through an online catalog or a law firm network.

Westlaw and Lexis both currently provide access to the same legal journal index database, *Legal Resources Index*, which is similar to the print *Current Law Index*. This online journal index does not index any articles prior to 1980. Although the index itself does not contain the full text of articles, if Westlaw or Lexis has the full text of a particular article, the index entry will link to the article within that service. Currently, Bloomberg does not include an index of law review and journal articles.

B. Finding Full-Text Articles on Westlaw, Lexis, and Bloomberg

Most researchers opt to search the full text of law review and journal articles using keyword searching on Westlaw and Lexis; both provide large databases of full-text law review and journal articles. Bloomberg provides a significantly smaller database of articles. You should check the scope note for the database to learn about the chronological coverage of the database and to learn how the content might otherwise be limited.

Many researchers who search the full-text databases of law review and journal articles on Westlaw, Lexis, or Bloomberg mistakenly believe they have done a comprehensive search. But Westlaw and Lexis include more articles in their indexes than they make available in full-text. Therefore, searching only the full-text database of one of these services is not as thorough as searching the online index, because (1) full-text coverage for many law reviews and journals did not begin until the 1990s, and (2) even after full-text coverage did begin, the coverage was likely selective rather than comprehensive.

There are also other differences between searching the indexes and searching the full-text databases. Each index record includes bibliographic information such as the title, author, date of publication, etc. But the index editors add subject headings—standardized language that may not appear in the title (or text)—that might better match your search terms. Alternatively, the full-text databases, while more limited in content, allow you to search every word in every article in each database. However, there are no subject headings or standardized language added to the full-text databases. Which source is better depends on your research needs; knowing the differences between the two search strategies will help you make a better decision.

C. HeinOnline

HeinOnline is a database that contains the searchable full text of all articles from each volume of most law reviews and journals, beginning with the first volume (unlike the databases on Lexis and Westlaw, where coverage begins with volumes published in the 1980s). In HeinOnline, you can also browse the table of contents for each volume. Most importantly, all the pages are available as PDF images, which many researchers find more comfortable to read online and easier to cite correctly. HeinOnline is a subscription product available at law school libraries and increasingly available in law firms.

D. Internet Sites

Google Scholar searches many scholarly databases with Google's powerful search engine, including several databases that include law review and journal articles (such as HeinOnline). It is a free service provided by Google, but it does not include access to the articles unless they are freely available on the Internet. Google Scholar provides links to allow you to purchase the articles and partners with academic libraries to integrate links to materials purchased by the libraries. Thus, when you are researching on a campus network, Google Scholar will recognize your location and provide access through the library's subscription. You can also set up this relationship via the "Library Links" tab that appears in the drop-down menu under Google Scholar's settings tab.

Another Internet option is the free full-text online law review and journal search engine maintained by the Law Technology group of the American Bar Association.[3] This search engine focuses more narrowly on the free full text of more than 300 online law reviews and journals. Still, the same caveats apply with regard to the comprehensiveness of a search using this search engine.

SSRN (formerly known as the Social Science Research Network)[4] and Digital Commons[5] provide free access to articles written by legal scholars. The authors themselves post selected published articles and works-in-progress on these sites, so the coverage is not comprehensive (although some scholars have posted their entire body of work). Both sites allow you to search by keyword, author, title, and subject.

Many law schools' law reviews and journals have websites where the editors post the current tables of contents from recent issues. Some law reviews and journals even post the full text of recent issues. A few post substantial collections of law review and journal issues in repositories accessible via their webpages. Although these issues are available for free, the quantity and variety of the articles posted has typically been inconsistent and irregular enough to make these websites unreliable as a first choice when you are looking for law review and journal articles. However, using such websites may be a good approach if you

3. lawtechnologytoday.org/free-full-text-online-law-review-journal-search.
4. ssrn.com/en/.
5. bepress.com/products/digital-commons/.

are seeking a specific recent article from a specific law review or journal. Table 3-4 shows the current links to law review and journal repositories at several North Carolina law schools.

Table 3-4. Law Review & Journal Repositories of North Carolina Law Schools

Campbell	scholarship.law.campbell.edu/clr/
Duke	law.duke.edu/scholarship/journals/
Elon	elon.edu/e/law/law-review/
NCCU	archives.law.nccu.edu/peer_review_list.html
UNC	archives.law.unc.edu/peer_review_list.html
Wake Forest	wakeforestlawreview.com/

Printing is an option from most of these online services, but due to the length of most law review and journal articles, printing them on demand can be expensive, environmentally unsound, or both. Consider downloading the articles instead.

E. Other Types of Legal Periodicals

Most state bar organizations publish a bar journal. The North Carolina State Bar publishes the *North Carolina Bar Journal,* a quarterly magazine providing a wide array of articles related to law practice and professionalism in North Carolina. It also contains bar-related notices such as bar committee actions, ethics opinions, disciplinary actions, and rule amendments. The *Bar Journal* is distributed to lawyers licensed to practice in North Carolina. Selected articles published after 2000 may be freely available via a search screen from the North Carolina Bar website.[6] The *Bar Journal* is useful to practicing attorneys for current awareness purposes as well as to practitioners and researchers for its valuable articles.

At the national level, several fee-based legal newspapers with associated websites contain a combination of free and fee-based information. Examples include the *National Law Journal*[7] and the *New York Law Journal.*[8] There are also several legal news websites, such as *Law.com*[9] and *FindLaw Legal News.*[10]

6. ncbar.gov/news-publications/the-journal/.
7. nationallawjournal.com.
8. newyorklawjournal.com.
9. law.com.
10. legalnews.findlaw.com.

An example of a North Carolina legal periodical serving a current awareness role is *North Carolina Lawyers Weekly*, a weekly printed newspaper also published at a website updated daily.[11] The website contains news about North Carolina cases and statutes as well as news about North Carolina lawyers, law firms, and cases. *Lawyers Weekly* contains a mixture of free and fee-based information of interest to researchers and practitioners.

V. American Law Reports

American Law Reports (A.L.R.) is a "hybrid" publication;[12] its name suggests that it is a case reporter, but in many ways, it functions more like a legal encyclopedia. A.L.R. contains important cases (selected by the editors at West Publishing) accompanied by Annotations written by attorneys. A.L.R. is now in its seventh series, though Annotations from earlier series can still be very useful research tools. *A.L.R. Federal* is a separate set that focuses only on federal law. *A.L.R. International* is another separate set that focuses on issues of worldwide importance, including international law topics.

The value of A.L.R. lies not in the cases it reports but in the accompanying Annotations—essays that are sometimes the same length as law review articles. These Annotations are narrow in scope; they typically address legal issues that are the subject of some controversy or that are interpreted differently across the United States. An Annotation usually describes in depth the various interpretations of a point of law throughout the United States, with the different states grouped together according to similarities in their interpretations of the relevant law.

In addition to describing the law, A.L.R. Annotations provide citations to primary authority and links to other recommended secondary sources, such as legal encyclopedias and law review and journal articles. Because of these references, many researchers find the Annotations especially useful at the beginning of their research process. A.L.R. does not attempt to cover American law comprehensively, like a legal encyclopedia does; thus, there is not an Annotation directly on point for every legal topic. However, if an A.L.R. Annotation exists for your topic, it can be a gold mine of relevant information.

Each Annotation has its own Table of Contents, making it relatively easy to locate the relevant portions of the Annotation. Most Annotations also contain lists of cases on specific fact patterns; those lists are arranged by the outcomes

11. nclawyersweekly.com.

12. J.D.S. Armstrong, Christopher A. Knott, & R. Martin Witt, *Where the Law Is: An Introduction to Advanced Legal Research* 133 (5th ed. 2018).

of the cases. For example, assume you are working on an age discrimination case that turns on the issue of constructive discharge. A relevant A.L.R. Annotation would provide a list of cases whose particular facts were held to be a constructive discharge and a list of cases whose facts were held not to be a constructive discharge.[13] Analyzing the cases in these lists will help you understand how the rules governing constructive discharge have been applied in various jurisdictions.

Another useful feature of an A.L.R. Annotation is the Table of Cases, which is broken down by jurisdiction (federal and state). If the Annotation mentions any North Carolina cases that discuss the narrow question the Annotation addresses, the Table will provide the citations to those cases and will direct you to the subsections of the Annotation in which those cases are treated. In this way, A.L.R. can be a state-specific research tool.

The process of researching in A.L.R. involves using relevant search terms to search the index and locate Annotations addressing your specific legal question. When searching A.L.R. in print, use the multi-volume hardbound Index. This Index includes Annotations from *A.L.R. Federal*. For relatively simple, straightforward questions, you might try the one-volume paperback *A.L.R. Quick Index*. A separate one-volume paperback, *A.L.R. Federal* Quick Index, is also available.

Like case reporters, A.L.R. is a serial publication; new volumes of *A.L.R.* and *A.L.R. Federal* containing new Annotations are issued throughout the year. Each individual A.L.R. volume is updated annually with a cumulative supplement (pocket part) containing cases decided since the publication of the volume. For this reason, an older A.L.R. Annotation can be just as helpful as a newer one; you should consult any A.L.R. Annotation that discusses your legal question, regardless of when it was originally published.

Westlaw and Lexis both have A.L.R. databases that include A.L.R. through its seventh series and *A.L.R. Federal* through its third series. The databases are updated weekly with new case Annotations. The databases include the multi-volume Index as well as electronic Annotations that are not yet released for print publication.

---

13. See Alan G. Skutt, Annotation, *Circumstances Which Warrant Finding of Constructive Discharge in Cases under Age Discrimination in Employment Act (29 U.S.C.A. §621 et seq.)*, 93 A.L.R. Fed. 10 (1989).

VI. Restatements and Principles

Restatements are summaries ("restatements") of the law in traditionally common law subject areas such as contracts, torts, and property. Restatements were developed because no unifying, broadly applicable statements of law for these subjects existed; many cases had to be read together in a time-consuming manner to understand the applicable law. Restatements set out the applicable legal rules in a format that resembles statutes. They also include official commentary on how the rules should be interpreted, examples (called *illustrations*) of how the rules work in various factual situations, and summaries of cases (published in a separate appendix volume) that apply and interpret the rules. *Principles*, introduced in the 1990s, are summaries of what the drafters believe the law should be in certain areas.

A. How Restatements and Principles are Created

Restatements and Principles are crafted by a group or committee of scholars, judges, and practitioners commissioned by the American Law Institute. The lead scholars for each Restatement and each Principle are called *reporters*, and the other drafters are called *associate reporters* or *advisers*. The reporters organize the work of the committee in producing a document that summarizes the existing law. The painstaking process of creating the drafts leading up to a final Restatement or Principle and the respect earned by the reporters and members of the committee all contribute to the high regard in which Restatements and Principles are held. Among secondary sources, Restatements are generally regarded as the most authoritative. If the North Carolina Supreme Court or the North Carolina Court of Appeals has cited a provision of a Restatement as support for a legal rule, that provision carries great persuasive weight in legal documents submitted to North Carolina courts.

Restatements and Principles are published by subject. A complete up-to-date list of subjects is available at the American Law Institute's website.[14] Within each Restatement subject are series, some of which first began in the 1920s. Currently, third series Restatements are being published. Subjects have been added since the first series subjects in the 1920s. It is possible that a Restatement on a subject may be drafted and published for the first time as a second series or a third series, when no previous Restatement for that subject exists in earlier series. See Tables 3-5 and 3-6 below for lists of Restatement subjects and Principles subjects, respectively.

14. ali.org/publications.

Table 3-5. Restatement Subjects[15]

Agency	Property (Landlord and Tenant)
American Indians	Property (Mortgages)
Charitable Non-Profit Organizations	Property (Servitudes)
Children and the Law	Property (Wills and Other Donative Transfers)
Conflict of Laws	Restitution and Unjust Enrichment
Consumer Contracts	Suretyship and Guaranty
Contracts	Torts
Employment Law	Torts: Apportionment of Liability
Foreign Relations Law of the United States	Torts: Intentional Torts to Persons
U.S. Law of International Commercial and Investment Arbitration	Torts: Liability for Economic Harm
Judgments	Torts: Liability for Physical and Emotional Harm
The Law Governing Lawyers	Torts: Product Liability
Liability Insurance	Trusts
	Unfair Competition

Table 3-6. Principles Subjects

Aggregate Litigation	Intellectual Property: Principles Governing Jurisdiction, Choice of Law, and Judgments in Transnational Disputes
Corporate Governance: Analysis and Recommendations	Policing
Election Administration: Non-Precinct Voting and Resolution of Ballot-Counting Disputes	Software Contracts
Family Dissolution: Analysis and Recommendations	Student Sexual Misconduct: Procedural Frameworks for Colleges and Universities
Government Ethics	Transnational Civil Procedure
	Transnational Insolvency

15. There are also Concise Restatements of the Law Governing Lawyers, Torts, and Donative Transfers and Trusts.

B. Researching a Legal Question in the Restatements or Principles

To begin researching using print Restatements or Principles, start with the name of the legal subject you need to research (contracts or employment law, for example). Locate the multi-volume set for that subject and look for the index in the last volume before the appendix of cases. Although the text of Restatements and Principles may be updated only every few decades, the cases that cite the Restatements or Principles are updated at least once a year and are presented in cumulative pocket parts in the back of the volumes.

Restatements and Principles can be found online on Westlaw and Lexis. For example, in Westlaw, when you begin to type "restatement" in the universal search bar, a list of the Restatement-related databases appears. You can also access the Restatements and Principles via the Secondary Sources database. Many of the Restatement subjects are also available as individual databases.

Because the text of the Restatements and Principles is so slowly updated, they are not the best sources of information when you are researching new or cutting-edge legal issues. Their value lies in the certainty of the basic information comprising these topics.

VII. Continuing Legal Education Publications

Every state requires each attorney licensed to practice within that state to participate in a certain number of hours of classes each year to learn new or updated information about a particular area of the law. These classes are usually referred to as *continuing legal education* (CLE). Presenters and teachers at these classes often publish their course materials or make them available to attorneys and the public. CLE materials are typically very practical in nature; they often discuss either how the law has recently changed or how a legal process or procedure might be improved or better accomplished. CLE materials have current awareness value and may also be useful for a researcher who is unfamiliar with the issues related to a legal subject.

The CLE-sponsoring organization—often the state bar association, a state law school, or a special organization created to oversee or provide CLE courses—is usually responsible for publishing the information. For example, in North Carolina, both the Continuing Legal Education Office of the North Carolina Bar and the North Carolina Bar Association coordinate courses for attorneys and provide publications. The University of North Carolina School of Law Office of Continuing Legal Education produces an annual CLE event, the Festival of Legal Learning, covering a variety of topics. The other North Carolina law schools also offer CLE events periodically. Many CLE materials can be found in the law libraries of all six North Carolina law schools.

Several companies coordinate CLE events at the national level and publish course handbooks. For example, the Practising Law Institute (PLI) sells hundreds of publications from CLE programs via its website and provides access to a wide variety of OnDemand Web Programs.[16] Bloomberg provides many PLI publications as well as other CLE-type materials, accessible via various databases. Westlaw and Lexis also provide some CLE materials.

Again, like many secondary sources, CLE materials typically are not freely available on the Internet.

VIII. Legal Forms

For attorneys and law students who are preparing to draft a legal document—a contract, a will, a pleading, or even a brief to a court—a common research task is locating a helpful form to use as a go-by. Some legal forms serve more as "checklists" to ensure that your document contains the requisite components and uses proper terminology. Other legal forms are templates that you can download and complete electronically. Some forms are general, and some are jurisdiction- or proceeding-specific. Forms help lawyers and researchers avoid reinventing the wheel, saving time and resources. Moreover, there is comfort in knowing that a particular form has been used successfully in the past.

The key to using forms successfully is to select the correct (or most applicable) form. There are publications that either include forms or are composed entirely of forms. Some of these publications also include citations to primary authorities that support the use of each form. A number of form books are available in academic law libraries. Some forms are also available online, giving practitioners the ability to complete the forms online or to cut and paste portions of them into word processing software.

Almost every jurisdiction has forms that are specific to the laws and procedures of that jurisdiction. Some state-specific collections of forms do not contain the same number and variety of forms as the national form books; however, the forms available in a state-specific set are more relevant to the

16. pli.edu.

unique laws and procedures of that jurisdiction. In North Carolina, the classic form book is *Douglas' Forms*, a five-volume set containing forms addressing a wide range of legal issues. The print set is best approached by using the index at the end of the last volume. *Douglas' Forms* is also available on Lexis. Several North Carolina treatises include a set of forms specific to particular areas of North Carolina law. The North Carolina Administrative Office of the Courts also provides hundreds of civil and criminal procedure forms at the North Carolina Judicial Branch website.[17]

West's Legal Forms and *American Jurisprudence Pleading and Practice Forms Annotated* are examples of national form books. These and other national form books are available online from Westlaw and Lexis. Although not focused on a particular jurisdiction, these form books are very detailed and provide forms that can be adapted to nearly any situation. However, every attorney carries the burden of knowing and understanding exactly what is required in his jurisdiction and to meet his client's needs.

A number of commercial vendors provide legal forms via the Internet, such as U.S. Legal Forms[18] and FindLaw Forms.[19] These vendors' forms typically are not free, but they usually cost less than a licensed attorney would charge to prepare the correct form or document. These forms tend to be general in nature but might profess to be appropriate for various jurisdictions. Westlaw, Lexis, and Bloomberg all have large collections of forms and sample documents online. These forms are searchable and browsable by topic and jurisdiction.

If you work at a law firm or other legal organization, you may have access to a form bank maintained by the firm or organization. There is no need to spend time searching one of the above sources to find a form when you can simply consult a form bank where the attorneys in your own firm or organization have deposited usable forms. (Some law firms and organizations also maintain brief banks, where associated members can access a previous researcher's work on a legal topic and simply update the work that was done on the original brief or memorandum.)

17. nccourts.gov/documents/forms.
18. uslegalforms.com.
19. forms.lp.findlaw.com.

IX. Jury Instructions

When conducting a jury trial, a judge typically asks the lawyers (before or during the trial) for their proposed jury instructions. Attorneys preparing for a jury trial will often need to research the pattern jury instructions for their jurisdiction and select the ones most relevant or favorable to their client's case.

The University of North Carolina School of Government began publishing the *North Carolina Pattern Jury Instructions* in the 1960s. These instructions are now compiled and updated by the Committee on Pattern Jury Instructions of the North Carolina Conference of Superior Court Judges along with the Institute of Government. The instructions are updated every year. The pattern jury instructions available in North Carolina are as follows:

- North Carolina Pattern Jury Instructions for Civil Cases
- North Carolina Pattern Jury Instructions for Criminal Cases
- North Carolina Pattern Jury Instructions for Motor Vehicle Cases

North Carolina Pattern Jury Instructions are available from several sources: (1) from the Institute of Government as a free download in PDF format (as of 2015);[20] (2) from the Institute of Government by subscription in software or hard copy format; (3) online through Fastcase and Casemaker (Fastcase is available to North Carolina Bar Association Members at no additional cost); and (4) digitally from the CX Corporation as a freestanding desktop application.[21] Be sure to check for the latest updates, which are distributed annually.

Federal model jury instructions are available in many libraries and are designed to explain relevant issues of federal law to a jury trying a federal case.

X. Uniform Laws and Model Acts

The Uniform Law Commission[22] is an organization that drafts and publishes uniform laws and model codes; its stated goal is to "provide[] states with non-partisan, well-conceived and well-drafted legislation that brings clarity and stability" to areas of state statutory law where "uniformity is desirable and practical."[23]

---

20. sog.unc.edu/resources/microsites/north-carolina-pattern-jury-instructions.
21. ncpji.com (for registered users).
22. uniformlaws.org.
23. uniformlaws.org/aboutulc/overview.

Each state is responsible for selecting judges, jurists, professors, and legislators to serve on the Commission. The commissioners attend the national meetings of the Commission to work on preparing and adopting the uniform laws and model codes. In addition to drafting the proposed statutory language of the law or code, the Commission also publishes explanatory notes and comments about the proposed law or code. Perhaps the most prominent example of the Commission's work is the Uniform Commercial Code, which has been enacted into law, in whole or in part, by all fifty states. Another well-known product of the Commission's work is the Model Penal Code, which is a staple of most first-year criminal law classes.

A uniform law or model code is especially useful in jurisdictions that have adopted that law or code. Though a jurisdiction is free to make any changes it deems appropriate when adopting the proposed law or code, the Commission's explanatory notes are often helpful to courts and attorneys who need to interpret or better understand the provisions at issue. At the Uniform Law Commission's website there is a map for each uniform law and model code showing which jurisdictions have adopted that law or code.[24]

The most widely available print publication of the Commission's work is a West publication called *Uniform Laws Annotated, Master Edition* (ULA); the volumes in this set are updated annually with cumulative pocket parts. You can locate the print ULA in your library's online catalog. The uniform laws are also available online on Westlaw and Lexis.

XI. Law-Related Blogs

A wide variety of legal commentary is available on law-related blogs, sometimes called "blawgs." Legal blogs are usually only as valuable as the reputations of the authors. Blog commentary from a recognized expert in a legal area could assist a researcher in the same way that commentary from a treatise might. Even commentary from less well-known blog authors could provide useful information when you are researching a topic. But because blogs are often not edited, you must filter through a great deal of commentary and make your own assessment of the value and quality of the information. This is a common problem when using free resources found on the Internet. An-

24. uniformlaws.org.

other problem that sometimes arises when you are researching on law-related blogs is using too much time to find information of little relevance.

Potential blog authors or topics can be identified using a search engine such as Google. However, perhaps the best approach to finding quality law-related blogs is to use the Blawg Directory at the American Bar Association Journal website.[25] Currently, the directory is browsable by topic, author type, region, law school, and courts. The Directory is continuously updated.

With regard to North Carolina specifically, a quick Google search will lead you to blogs on many different subjects, including appellate practice, criminal law, family law, construction law, and traffic law.

XII. Tools for the Toolbox

1. Consider using secondary sources when
   a. you are researching an area of the law you are unfamiliar with.
   b. you are having difficulty finding primary authority.
   c. you are researching an area of the law that is new or undeveloped.
   d. you need guidance in sifting through a large amount of primary authority.
2. Before relying on a secondary source, carefully assess its quality and credibility.
3. When you use a secondary source to find primary authority, always read the primary authority yourself before relying on it.
4. In general, do not cite to secondary authority unless there is little or no relevant primary authority or the secondary authority is widely regarded as reliable and persuasive (e.g., Restatements).

25. abajournal.com/blawgs.

Table 3-7. Summary of Key Characteristics of Secondary Sources

	What does this source contain?	Who authors or compiles this source?	Why would you use this source?	What is the best method for researching in this source?
Legal Encyclopedias	• General overview of the law on a variety of topics. • Typically multi-volume publications that organize information alphabetically by topic. • Limited citations to primary authority.	• Usually authored by attorneys who are well-versed in the specific topics.	• To locate background information on a topic. • To help you focus your research and guide you to primary authorities as well as other relevant secondary authorities.	• Search in the Westlaw and/or Lexis databases (these provide the easiest access and the most up-to-date information).
Treatises and Hornbooks	Some or all of the following: • a review of how the law on a topic has developed; • an explanation of the legal rules on the topic; • an analysis of key statutes and cases on the topic; • a discussion of policy questions on the topic; • citations to primary and secondary authority on the topic.	• Usually authored by law professors.	• To find in-depth treatment of a specific area of the law. • To point you to primary authorities on a specific legal topic.	• Consult a law librarian or law professor to identify treatises or hornbooks in a particular area of law. • Locate them in the online catalog of your law library (most treatises and hornbooks are not available on commercial platforms or on the Internet). • Limited availability in Westlaw, Lexis, and Bloomberg.
Periodicals (law reviews and journals)	• Heavily footnoted scholarly articles that analyze, compare, and/or critique the law in a specific area and sometimes suggest changes to the law.	• Articles are usually authored by law professors or experienced, knowledgeable practitioners. • Student editors also write articles, called notes or comments.	• To learn how the law in a particular area has developed. • To help you find primary and other secondary authorities related to the topic you are researching.	• Online indexes. • Search in the Westlaw & Lexis databases. • HeinOnline. • SSRN and/or Digital Commons.

A.L.R. Annotations	• Selected cases with accompanying Annotations, usually involving legal questions that are the subject of some controversy or that are interpreted differently across the United States. • Annotations describe the law, provide citations to primary authority and links to other recommended secondary sources.	• Usually written by attorneys who practice in the relevant subject areas.	• To get an overview of an area of law. • To learn how different jurisdictions have interpreted the law on a particular narrow legal question. • To help you find other primary and secondary authorities related to the legal question you are researching.	• Search in the Westlaw and/or Lexis databases.
Restatements	• Summaries ("restatements") of the law in traditionally common law subject areas such as contracts, torts, and property. • Include (1) the applicable legal rules in a format that resembles statutes; (2) official commentary on how the rules should be interpreted; (3) examples (*illustrations*) of how the rules work in various factual situations; (4) summaries of cases that apply and interpret the rules.	• Written by a group or committee of scholars, judges, and practitioners (called *reporters*) under the umbrella of the American Law Institute.	• To read a summary of the existing law on a particular legal topic. • To find authority to support a proposition (the Restatement may reference primary authority from your jurisdiction or provide persuasive authority).	• Search in the Westlaw and/or Lexis databases.

Chapter Four

Constitutions and Statutes

Within the category of primary authority, *constitutions* and *statutes* are of chief importance; if there are constitutional or statutory provisions that govern your research question, it is critically important to find and understand those provisions early in your research process. *Constitutions* provide the fundamental governing principles for a nation or state. *Statutes* are written laws created and enacted by legislative bodies.

I. Constitutions

Constitutions provide the fundamental governing principles for many nations, including the United States, and for individual states within the United States. In the United States, the United States Constitution is the supreme law of the land, and all other laws, federal and state, must be consistent with its provisions. In North Carolina, the North Carolina Constitution provides the fundamental governing principles under which all branches of the state government must operate and details the individual liberties to which North Carolina citizens are entitled. "A state's constitution may grant greater rights than those secured by the federal constitution, but because a state's constitution is subordinate to the federal constitution, it cannot provide lesser rights than those secured by the federal constitution."[1]

In the next two sections of this chapter, we outline the various tools that assist researchers in locating and interpreting provisions of the North Carolina Constitution and the United States Constitution, respectively.

1. Amy E. Sloan, *Basic Legal Research: Tools and Strategies* 2 (14th ed. Aspen 2018).

A. The North Carolina Constitution

1. History and Scope

The North Carolina Constitution currently in effect is the third version of the document. The first version was drafted and adopted in 1776, and the second version was adopted in 1868. The current version of the North Carolina Constitution was adopted in 1971. Professor John Orth's essay on the North Carolina Constitution is a good primer for those interested in North Carolina's constitutional history.[2]

The North Carolina Constitution currently contains fourteen articles, as detailed in Table 4-1.

Table 4-1. Articles of the North Carolina Constitution

Article I.	Declaration of Rights
Article II.	Legislative
Article III.	Executive
Article IV.	Judicial
Article V.	Finance
Article VI.	Suffrage and Eligibility to Office
Article VII.	Local Government
Article VIII.	Corporations
Article IX.	Education
Article X.	Homesteads and Exemptions
Article XI.	Punishments, Corrections, and Charities
Article XII.	Military Forces
Article XIII.	Conventions; Constitutional Amendment and Revision
Article XIV.	Miscellaneous

2. Researching the North Carolina Constitution

The North Carolina Constitution is available in the two print versions of the North Carolina statutory code, *West's North Carolina Statutes Annotated* (published by West) and *The General Statutes of North Carolina Annotated* (published by LexisNexis). In each version, the Constitution is published in a

2. Available at ncpedia.org/government/nc-constitution-history.

separate volume and is indexed in the general index of the set. Along with the text of the Constitution, both versions of the code contain research annotations, such as summaries of citations to court decisions that have discussed and interpreted the Constitution. The annotations may also include historical and statutory notes, related opinions of the Attorney General, and citations to related law review or journal articles.

The North Carolina Constitution is also available on Westlaw, Lexis, and Bloomberg. All of these online resources allow you to search the Constitution by running a keyword search or by browsing the table of contents. Westlaw and Lexis provide the same research annotations that appear in their print publications. Westlaw also offers a *North Carolina Constitution Find Template* that allows you to locate North Carolina Constitution provisions using the statute article and section number. Bloomberg, however, includes only the text of the current North Carolina Constitution; it does not have annotations.

The current North Carolina Constitution is also available for free on the North Carolina General Assembly website.[3] The North Carolina Legislative Library website provides links to previous versions of the Constitution and to the amendments from 1873 to present, all of which are accessible for free.[4] However, the version of the North Carolina Constitution on the General Assembly website lacks the annotations and editorial enhancements available in the Westlaw and Lexis versions.

3. Interpreting the North Carolina Constitution

A helpful book for interpreting the North Carolina Constitution is *The North Carolina State Constitution*.[5] This book provides a section-by-section analysis of the current North Carolina Constitution as well as an overview of the drafting and ratification process of all three versions of the Constitution.

If you determine that the previous versions of the North Carolina Constitution would be useful in understanding and interpreting the current version, you can find them in several sources. The North Carolina Constitution of 1776 is available in the 1909 classic publication, *The Federal and State Constitutions, Colonial Charters and Other Organic Laws of the States, Territories and Colonies*

3. www.ncleg.gov/Laws/Constitution.

4. ncleg.gov/library/Research/nc%20research/constitution.html.

5. John V. Orth & Paul Martin Newby, *The North Carolina State Constitution* (2d ed. 2013). This book is part of the Oxford Commentaries on the State Constitutions of the United States. *See also* John V. Orth, *The Law of the Land: The North Carolina Constitution and State Constitutional Law*, 70 N.C. L. Rev. 1759 (1992).

Now or Heretofore Forming the United States of America, compiled and edited by Francis Newton Thorpe.[6] For a more comprehensive treatment of North Carolina colonial documents and sources of the 1776 North Carolina Constitution, see Chapter 35, "North Carolina Colonial Legal Materials," in *Pre-Statehood Legal Materials, A Fifty State Research Guide*.[7] The 1776 North Carolina Constitution is also conveniently available online at the Avalon Project, Lillian Goldman Law Library, Yale Law School.[8]

B. The United States Constitution

1. Researching the United States Constitution

Like the North Carolina Constitution, the United States Constitution is available in both print and online formats. The print version of the official federal statutory code, the *United States Code*, includes the unannotated text of the United States Constitution. Fortunately, the Constitution is also included in both print versions of the annotated United States Code, West's *United States Code Annotated* and Lexis's *United States Code Service*. It is also included in both print versions of North Carolina's statutory code, Lexis's *General Statutes of North Carolina Annotated* and West's *North Carolina General Statutes Annotated*.

The United States Constitution is also available on Westlaw, Lexis, and Bloomberg and can be searched by browsing the table of contents or by performing a keyword search. The versions on Westlaw and Lexis contain both the text and annotations; the annotations include citations to relevant cases interpreting constitutional provisions and references to secondary sources. The version on Bloomberg contains only the text.

The United States Constitution is also available online at no cost. The U.S. Government Publishing Office (GPO) information website contains *The Constitution of the United States of America: Analysis and Interpretation* (popularly known as the Constitution Annotated).[9] This resource provides legal analysis and interpretation of the United States Constitution with in-text annotations of cases decided by the United States Supreme Court.

---

6. Government Printing Office, 1909, under Act of Congress June 30, 1906.

7. This resource is edited by Michael Chiorazzi and Marguerite Most and published by Haworth Press, 2006.

8. avalon.law.yale.edu/18th_century/nc07.asp.

9. govinfo.gov/collection/constitution-annotated.

2. Interpreting the United States Constitution

The United States Constitution is the subject of an exponential number of interpretive texts and treatises. Using one of these texts or treatises during your research will prove to be very beneficial. Preeminent treatises include Rotunda and Nowak's *Treatise on Constitutional Law—Substance & Procedure*, 5th Edition, and Laurence Tribe's *American Constitutional Law*. Use a library's online catalog to locate additional texts and treatises interpreting the Constitution.

Many, many court opinions have interpreted provisions of the United States Constitution. If your research question involves one of its provisions, you should conduct a thorough search of case law to find relevant cases. Chapter 8 details how to research case law.

II. Statutes

Statutes are laws enacted by legislative bodies. Statutes are an important part of the legal hierarchy because they regulate many significant areas of the law. In addition to looking for constitutional provisions that govern your research question, you should always look for relevant statutory provisions. The remainder of this chapter will address how to research North Carolina and federal statutes, respectively. Chapter 5 will address how to research documents generated during the process of enacting statutes, collectively referred to as *legislative history*.

A. North Carolina Statutes

The North Carolina General Assembly, made up of the North Carolina Senate (Senate) and the North Carolina House of Representatives (House), is the legislative body that enacts statutes in North Carolina. The General Assembly meets in a regular session (the "long session") beginning in January of each odd-numbered year and reconvenes the following even-numbered year (the "short session").

1. Sources of North Carolina Statutes

A proposed statute, commonly called a *bill*, is enacted into law in North Carolina in a two-step process (with a few exceptions). First, it must be *ratified* (passed in identical form) by both chambers of the North Carolina General Assembly. Next, it is presented to the Governor for *approval*, usually on the day after ratification; if the Governor signs it, or takes no action, the bill become law and is thereafter referred to as a *session law.*

A few types of bills become law immediately upon ratification, with no gubernatorial approval needed. These include bills making appointments, proposing constitutional amendments, and revising districts.

a. Session Laws

Newly enacted statutes are called *session laws* because they were passed during a legislative session. Session laws are published chronologically, in the order in which they were passed in each session of the General Assembly. Session laws are not annotated; they contain only the text of the statute. North Carolina session laws can be found in several sources.

Session Laws of North Carolina, an annual print publication, is available at many state and academic law libraries in North Carolina. The State Library provides electronic access to session laws back to 1777.[10] Also, many academic law libraries across the country provide access to all fifty states' session laws either through an online service such as HeinOnline (which includes laws from 1715 forward, including the North Carolina Colony laws) or on microfiche.

The North Carolina General Assembly website[11] is an excellent free source of session laws. The site includes session laws dating back to the 1959–1960 General Assembly session.

Current North Carolina session laws can be found in print and online versions of the state statutory code, the North Carolina General Statutes, as discussed in the next section of this chapter. Print codes integrate session laws into the current statutory set using paper pamphlet supplements throughout the year; Westlaw and Lexis integrate session laws into their databases much more quickly.

b. The North Carolina Codes

Shortly after they are passed, session laws are integrated into a statutory code that is organized by subject. This step is often referred to as *codification.* Without codification, searching for relevant, current statutory law would be extremely difficult. Researchers need a tool that collects, groups by subject matter, and updates all statutes in one place. That tool is called a *code.*

North Carolina's statutory code is composed of chapters numbered up to 168. Each chapter is subdivided into subchapters, articles, and sections. For

10. ncgovdocs.org/guides/sessionlawslist.htm.

11. ncleg.gov

citation purposes, only the chapters and sections are used. For example, N.C. Gen. Stat. §42-45 refers to chapter 42, section 45 of the code.

There are two print editions of the North Carolina code. Lexis publishes the *official*[12] code, the *General Statutes of North Carolina Annotated*, and West publishes an *unofficial*[13] code, *West's North Carolina General Statutes Annotated*. Both publications annotate each section of the code with citations to cases interpreting that code section and summaries of those cases. The annotations also typically include citations to relevant secondary sources such as law review and journal articles, legal encyclopedias, and *American Law Reports* annotations. If you cannot start a research project with secondary sources and must start with a primary law source, an annotated statutory code would be the best starting point.

i. *General Statutes of North Carolina Annotated*

The official North Carolina code is Lexis's *General Statutes of North Carolina Annotated*. This version is published in twenty-five softbound volumes that are replaced every two years. The annotations in this version of the code include all decisions of the North Carolina Supreme Court and North Carolina Court of Appeals, all decisions in federal cases arising in North Carolina, state law reviews and journals, *American Law Reports* annotations, and North Carolina Attorney General opinions. The set also includes a separate, fully annotated softbound volume, *Annotated Rules of North Carolina*, containing an exhaustive list of court and practice rules.[14]

A two-volume Interim Supplement is used to update the set (both the statutes and the annotations) in non-replacement years. Lexis also provides *North Carolina Advance Annotation Service* (AAS) and General Statutes of *North Carolina Advance Legislative Service* (ALS) pamphlets. The AAS is published three times a year and provides case annotations covering recent decisions of (1) the North Carolina Supreme Court and Court of Appeals, (2) the Supreme Court of the United States, and (3) federal District Courts, Circuit Courts of Appeals, and bankruptcy courts that construe North Carolina law.

---

12. North Carolina has authorized Lexis to publish the statutes on its behalf; therefore, the General Statutes of North Carolina Annotated is the official version of the code. Amy E. Sloan, *Basic Legal Research: Tools and Strategies* 176–77 (7th ed. Aspen 2018).

13. An unofficial publication is published without government authorization. Thus, in the unlikely event that some discrepancy exists between the official and unofficial versions of the statute, the official version controls and constitutes the law. *Id.*

14. *See* Chapter 9 for more on North Carolina rules.

The ALS is published quarterly and contains the newest session laws passed by the General Assembly. Each pamphlet includes several tables to assist researchers, such as a Table of General Statutes Chapters with corresponding bill numbers from the newly passed session laws, and a reverse table of bills and the corresponding chapter numbers. The Table of Sections Added, Amended, or Appealed allows you to look up a specific *General Statutes* section number to determine whether any of the new session laws affect it. Finally, the ALS pamphlet includes a cumulative subject index.

Lexis provides complete access to the official contents of the *General Statutes of North Carolina Annotated* in a searchable online database. The database also contains a searchable and browsable table of contents with hyperlinked references.

A separate Lexis database is available for the Advance Legislative Service, which is continuously updated. The database includes session laws passed in the current legislative session (usually within a few days of passage) and covers all session laws dating back to 1989.

ii. *West's North Carolina General Statutes Annotated*

In 1999, West began publishing an unofficial but useful codification of the North Carolina General Statutes, *West's North Carolina General Statutes Annotated.* The statutory text is identical to that of the official version, as is the codification scheme. The annotations, however, differ somewhat between the two codes. The West code typically has more comprehensive case law annotations, called "Notes of Decisions." The West code also references the *North Carolina Administrative Code* and various analytical products, such as the West Topic and Key Number System and *Strong's North Carolina Index.*

The West code is published in hardbound volumes and is updated with annual pocket parts. The annual pocket parts are supplemented throughout the year with *Interim Update* pamphlets that update both the text of the code, as new session laws are passed by the General Assembly, and the annotations to the existing code. The new information is conveniently organized into the chapter arrangement of the code.

The West code is also updated with the *North Carolina Legislative Service,* published several times during each legislative session. In addition to providing the text of recently enacted session laws, the *Service* also includes a cumulative statutes table showing the sections of the code affected by the new session laws, a list of the House and Senate bills that became the enacted session laws, and a cumulative subject index.

Westlaw provides the complete contents of *West's North Carolina General Statutes Annotated* in a searchable online database. Like Lexis, Westlaw also provides the chapters in a table of contents form that permits convenient browsing of the code.

Westlaw includes tools such as a browsable Annotated Index and Popular Name Table and a North Carolina Statutes Find Template, which allows researchers to retrieve a statute by entering only the numeric portion of the citation.

c. Other Sources for North Carolina General Statutes

i. Bloomberg Law

Bloomberg maintains the text of the current North Carolina General Statutes in its database. However, it is not annotated like the versions on Westlaw and Lexis.

ii. North Carolina General Assembly Website

The North Carolina General Assembly website contains a free version of the North Carolina General Statutes.[15] This version of the code is both searchable and browsable by chapter, but several caveats are warranted when using the General Assembly website. First, the website warns researchers that the text of the General Statutes found at the site is not official; only the Lexis print version contains the official text of the code. Second, the code found at this site is not annotated beyond some basic legislative history citations to session laws associated with the current text of the statutes. Third, the General Statutes version at this site is updated only once a year, after the General Assembly session ends.

2. Researching North Carolina Statutes

The overall process for researching in the print and online versions of the North Carolina General Statutes is strikingly similar. The only exception is the availability of keyword searching via the online research platforms.

a. Using a Citation or Popular Name

If you are fortunate enough to have a statutory citation, simply look up the code section in the print code. For example, the citation N.C. Gen. Stat. § 42-45 refers to a statute that is codified in chapter 42, section 45. So you would find that statute by pulling the volume that contains chapter 42 and paging through the volume until you find section 45.

---

15. ncleg.gov.

On Westlaw and Lexis, you can use the universal search bar to find a statute by citation. You will likely get the best results if you enter the citation in *Bluebook* form. As previously indicated, Westlaw has a Statutes Find Template that allows you to retrieve a statute by entering only the numeric portion of the citation. Bloomberg requires the special citation format NCCODE. However, its citation lookup tool can help you retrieve a section even if the citation is incorrect.

If you do not have a statutory citation, but you have the popular name of a session law (e.g. the Midwifery Practice Act), you can find the act in the Popular Name Table in the print index volume of the code. The entry will provide basic information about the act, including the chapter and section where the act is codified. Westlaw has a Popular Name alphabetical listing that is accessed from the *North Carolina General Statutes Annotated* database search screen. Alternatively, the popular name could be searched as a phrase in the General Statutes database in Westlaw, Lexis, Bloomberg, or the General Assembly website.

b. Browsing the Index

Without a statutory citation or the popular name of a session law, you must use relevant search terms to search the North Carolina General Statutes.[16] With search terms in hand, use the latest index volumes to find citations to relevant code sections. Most indexes contain "see" or "see also" references directing you to other terms that are logically related to your search term. In that way, the index is a superior method of connecting your search terms to related subjects in the code. It is important to be patient and flexible when using the index. If your first term does not work, try a synonym or broader term.

Westlaw allows you to browse the index of *West's North Carolina General Statutes Annotated* online. This approach combines the convenience of online access with the value of a human-mediated index. Rather than retrieving only those results that match your exact search terms from a keyword search using terms and connectors, a search of the index will include terms that are not necessarily in the text of the statutes you are searching but that are logically associated with it. This provides a greater opportunity to find relevant docu-

16. See Chapter 2 for methods of developing search terms.

ments. This option is not available on Lexis, Bloomberg, or the General Assembly website.

c. Browsing the Table of Contents

If you have some understanding of the subject of your research question, an alternative to searching the index to find relevant statutory provisions is browsing the table of contents of the code to select the most relevant chapter(s). The chapter titles within the North Carolina General Statutes refer to broad subject areas, i.e., Criminal Law, Motor Vehicles, or Wills. If, for example, you were researching the validity of a will for a client, you could go directly to the code chapter entitled Wills and browse the subtopics of the specific section(s) related to this question. Therefore, the more information you have about the subject of law you are researching and the structure of the code, the more likely you are to be successful with this approach. In the hypothetical scenario above, you would most likely find the answer to your question under the subtopic labeled Article 1: Execution of Will.

A browsable table of contents is available online on Westlaw, Lexis, Bloomberg, and the General Assembly website. See Figure 4-1 below for the Westlaw Table of Contents on the topic of Wills.

Figure 4-1. Westlaw Table of Contents

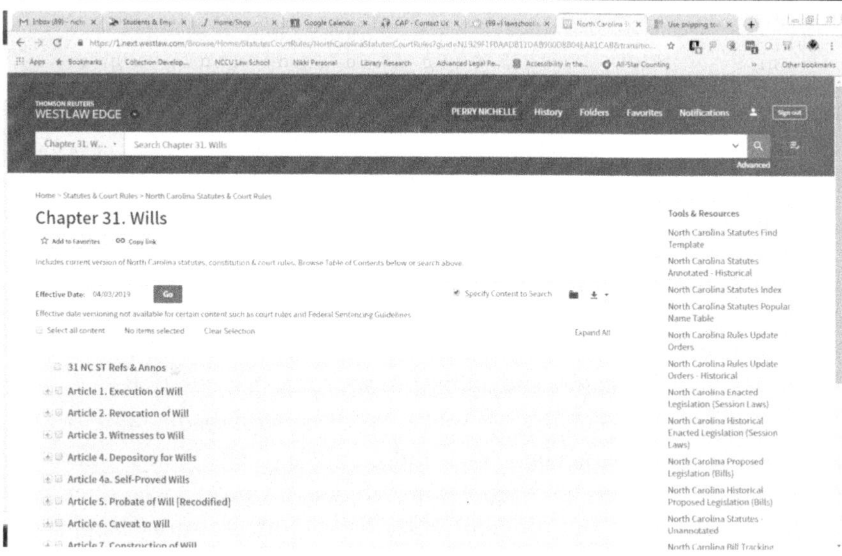

Source: Westlaw. Reprinted with permission of Thomson Reuters.

d. Keyword Searching

Statutes can also be located using keyword searches in the online databases. However, researching statutes online using keywords can be difficult. First, because legislatures use technical terms in statutes, you may miss a relevant statutory provision if you are not familiar with the statutory terminology. Second, in an online statutory search, you are searching every word in every document in the database. Thus, the best practice is to search the smallest database likely to have all of the relevant documents. If possible, you should narrow your keyword search to the specific chapters of the code you think will have relevant sections. The danger of this approach is that you might miss relevant sections hidden in unlikely chapters of the code. A thorough research process, such as the process discussed in this book, however, will decrease the chances of missing any relevant law.

On Westlaw, Lexis, and Bloomberg, you can use pre-search filters to limit the jurisdiction of your search to North Carolina and to limit the scope of your search to the statutory code only. Or you can simply select the North Carolina Statutes database on any of the platforms and run a well-designed search. In the databases on Westlaw and Lexis, the annotations are searched along with the text of the code. The case summaries and other annotations provide additional words related to your subject beyond the text of the statute to which your search terms will be exposed. This feature may enhance the quality of your retrieved results, though it also may result in a high number of irrelevant results.

The search engine at the General Assembly website offers few advanced search features compared to Westlaw, Lexis, and Bloomberg. In addition, the lack of annotations on the General Assembly website may hinder efficient searching. However, in those rare instances when searching the text alone (without annotations) is more efficient, the General Assembly website is a good choice.

e. Additional Code Research Strategies

After finding a potentially relevant statute, whether using a print code or researching online, follow the research strategy below. This strategy will help you understand the statute and apply it to your research question.

Reading statutory language is unlike any other legal reading task. Unlike a judicial decision written by a single judge or by a panel of judges, statutory law is created in a legislative process involving many people who often have different viewpoints and different objectives. Thus, statutory language is sometimes intentionally vague, so that the proposed statute will attract the largest number of supporters and be acceptable to the widest range of viewpoints. Statutory language can also be unintentionally vague as a result of inartful or careless drafting. In either case, vague statutory language opens the provision to various interpretations. A careful researcher will read a statute several times, to identify any ambiguities that require further research and interpretation.

There are two common strategies researchers use to understand and interpret statutory provisions, both of which relate to the context within which the provisions exist. The first strategy is to look for statutory definitions of words, especially those that are vague or ambiguous. Many statutes have separate definitions sections; consulting these sections will alert you to statutory terms that do not carry their everyday definitions. A simple way to locate a definitions section (if one exists) is to work backwards from the specific code section that contains the relevant provision (or scroll up, if you are working online) until you come to the beginning of the chapter or subchapter containing that provision. This is where most definitions sections appear. You can then skim the definitions section to determine whether it contains a definition of the term you are trying to interpret.

The second strategy is to spend a few minutes examining the context of an individual statutory provision by looking at the sections surrounding it (or perhaps by skimming the entire subchapter containing the section). Seeing how a provision fits into the larger statutory scheme can shed light on the purpose and meaning of the provision. Researchers often find that this examination is easier to conduct in the print versions of the code (where thumbing through pages is fairly easy) than online (where scrolling through numerous screens or following a trail of links can be tedious and time-consuming).

f. Using Case Annotations

No matter how carefully you read a statute, or how well you think you understand it, your research is not complete until you review any judicial decisions that have interpreted the statute. If a court in your jurisdiction has interpreted a code section, that interpretation must be either used or challenged; it cannot be ignored.

Both Westlaw and Lexis review cases and select a representative sample to include in the annotated versions of the North Carolina General Statutes (both in print and online). Both publishers attempt to include cases that represent all legal issues and novel factual interpretations of the code. Westlaw calls these cases "Notes of Decisions," while Lexis calls them "Case Notes." On Westlaw, they are included on a separate tab (do not confuse this with the "citing references" tab, which includes all cases and other sources that merely mention the code section). On Lexis, these appear after each code section. When using a print version of the code, be sure to examine the pocket parts and any supplementary pamphlets issued as part of the code to find notes about recent cases.

Remember that the summaries of cases within the annotated codes are not legal authority, but simply the editors' description or interpretation of the cases. Thus, if you determine that one or more cases summarized in the notes are relevant to your research question, be sure to locate and read each case, so that you have an accurate understanding of how it relates to the statutory provision that governs your research question.

If you are using an unannotated code (such as the ones found on the General Assembly's website and on Bloomberg), you will have to find the relevant cases yourself using the methods explained in Chapter 8.

B. Researching Statutes of Other States

Most states codify their statutes using some variant of the method used in North Carolina. Several states, including New York and Texas, publish their statutes in volumes by subject rather than by an overall numbering scheme. Nonetheless, the research strategies discussed in this chapter should be effective in those and other states as well.

Westlaw, Lexis, and Bloomberg provide convenient online access to all fifty states' codes, though this access can be expensive. Also, some academic law libraries still collect print versions of, or provide online access to, all fifty states' codes. Like North Carolina, many states provide an unofficial, unannotated version of their state's code on the Internet. Most states' free statutory codes may be retrieved using Google or another search engine. There are also some "mega" websites with convenient links to free legal information, including state statutory codes. Such sites include FindLaw[17] and Cornell's Legal Information Institute.[18]

---

17. findlaw.com.
18. law.cornell.edu.

C. Researching Federal Statutes

Federal statutes are researched in much the same way as state statutes. Laws that are enacted by the United States Congress are known as *public laws.*[19] They are first printed as *slip laws* (individually published acts of Congress). At the end of each legislative session, all slip laws from that session are published in *Statutes at Large*, which serves the same function as the *North Carolina Session Laws* publication. Next, the new statutes are codified and incorporated into the federal statutory code, the *United States Code*, which is arranged by subject.

Public laws are freely available almost immediately upon adoption on *govinfo*,[20] a website maintained by the Government Publishing Office. Public laws are also quickly available on Westlaw and Lexis. In the research process, public laws are of limited use because they serve only as snapshots of statutes as they were originally passed by Congress. A researcher usually needs to see the relevant statute in the context of other related statutes concerning that subject, and he also needs the most currently updated version of the statute. Therefore, rather than using *Statutes at Large* or public laws online for general statutory research, researchers often use one of the versions of the *United States Code*, described below. If, however, the research task involves finding an older version of a statute, or a provision that did not make it into the code (i.e., federal appropriations or temporary and private acts), *Statutes at Large* is a good place to start.

1. *United States Code*

The *United States Code* (U.S.C.) is the official federal statutory code, published by the government and arranged by subject into fifty-four titles. The U.S.C. is published every six years. In the intervening years, annual cumulative supplements are published that contain all changes to the code. The *United States Code* is available online in several places at no charge. Scans of the print U.S.C. (including supplements) are available on *govinfo.gov*. A more up-to-date version is available from the Office of Law Revision Council, the entity that creates the U.S.C.[21] The U.S.C. is also available from the Legal Information Institute.[22] Many courts require that documents submitted to them cite to the official U.S.C. for statutory provisions.

---

19. Occasionally, Congress enacts a Private Law, that is, a law that applies only to persons named in the law. These are published as slip laws and collected in the *Statutes at Large*. Private laws do not appear in the U.S. Code.

20. govinfo.gov/.

21. uscode.house.gov.

22. law.cornell.edu/uscode/text.

Typically, the supplements to the U.S.C. published by the government are several years out of date by the time they are issued. Practitioners cannot rely on information this old. Moreover, the U.S.C. is not annotated; it contains no citations to related secondary sources and no case summaries explaining how its provisions have been interpreted. Therefore, the official U.S.C. has limited usefulness in the research process.

Fortunately, several privately published versions of the *United States Code* are available to researchers whose research involves federal statutes. These codes are annotated and updated more often, among many benefits. The two leading annotated versions are the *United States Code Annotated* (U.S.C.A.), published by West, and the *United States Code Service* (U.S.C.S.), published by Lexis. Although they are unofficial codes, the statutory text of the U.S.C.A. and the U.S.C.S. should be identical to the text of the U.S.C.

Both annotated codes contain extensive summaries of cases interpreting the statutes (called Notes of Decision) and citations to those cases. They also include references to relevant regulations and to helpful secondary sources such as legal encyclopedias and A.L.R. annotations. There are some differences in the two versions, though. The U.S.C.A. includes references to appropriate Topic and Key Numbers from the West Digest System (discussed further in Chapter 7), which can be important in the research process. Also, the associated Topic and Key Numbers can be used to find relevant cases in all jurisdictions through the West Digest System either in print or on Westlaw. The U.S.C.S. includes more references to regulations for each section.

2. Research Strategies for Federal Statutes

The *United States Code Annotated* and the *United States Code Service* are both published in large print multi-volume sets. They are both updated by annual pocket parts placed in the back of each volume. Both publishers issue quarterly supplementary pamphlets providing updated text and case annotations. The updating process for both of these unofficial print versions includes examining the pocket parts as well as any supplementary pamphlets. Fortunately, these privately published versions are updated more regularly than the U.S.C.

The electronic versions of the *United States Code Annotated* and the *United States Code Service* are available on Westlaw and Lexis, respectively. An unannotated, but current, version of the *United States Code* is available on Bloomberg.

The following research strategies are applicable to both the U.S.C.A. and the U.S.C.S. unless otherwise noted.

a. Using the Citation or Popular Name

The easiest way to locate a statute is by its legal citation, such as 28 U.S.C. § 1331. To locate the statute, find the volumes containing title 28 and then find the individual volume that contains section 1331. On any of the online research platforms, you can enter a *United States Code* citation in the main search box of the home screen to retrieve a specific U.S.C. section.

A second way to locate a statute is by its popular name. Both annotated codes have a Popular Name Table that lists the Public Law number, the *Statutes at Large* citation, and the title and section number(s) where the statute is codified.[23] Remember that when a law is passed by a legislature, it may affect many different areas of the law and, therefore, may be codified in many different titles of the code.

Westlaw, Lexis, and Bloomberg all have searchable and browsable Popular Name Tables. On Westlaw, the table is located on the United States Code Annotated screen in the "Tools and Resources" column. On Lexis, researchers must use the search box on the home page to search for the "U.S.C.S. Popular Name Table" to bring up the table. Bloomberg has a link to the table at the bottom of its *United States Code* search page.

b. Searching the Index

Often you must look for relevant statutes without knowing a citation or popular name. In this instance, the most common method of locating relevant statutes is to use the index to locate the subject of your research question in the *United States Code*. The index is finely detailed; for example, a statute concerning the prevention of juvenile crime would be indexed under *juvenile* (the term used in the statute), as well as under related terms such as *child, youth, adolescent,* and *teen*. The index is also updated throughout the year.

Westlaw and Lexis provide electronic access to the code's index, combining the convenience of online access with the value of human intelligence. On Westlaw, the U.S.C.A. index is available on the U.S.C.A. screen in the "Tools and Resources" column. On Lexis, search for the U.S.C.S. index in the main search box or in the "Search for a Source" box. Bloomberg does not provide access to the code's index.

23. The Popular Name Table is published in a separate volume for all editions of the code.

c. Browsing Titles and the Table of Contents

Another way to research statutes is to simply select the appropriate title and volume from the shelf and browse the table of contents. This approach is usually more successful when you have substantial familiarity with the code and an understanding of the area of law you are researching. Also, this approach is easier when researching some legal issues than others. For example, when researching a copyright problem, you might know that the copyright statutes are contained in Title 17. However, some legal subjects are included in titles that are not immediately apparent from the titles' names, and some legal subjects are spread throughout several titles.

Researchers can browse and search the code's table of contents on Westlaw, Lexis, and Bloomberg. This method of searching allows the researcher to see related chapters and sections in context for a better understanding of how a relevant code section fits within the statutes covering a legal topic.

d. Searching the Code Online by Keyword

Westlaw, Lexis, and Bloomberg allow for full-text keyword searching. However, using keyword searching to retrieve code sections online can be extremely difficult. A word search in a database containing annotations will search both the statutory language and the annotations unless you specifically limit your search to words in the statute itself. It is best to limit your search to the *United States Code* or the smallest set of the *United States Code* that you believe will have all of the relevant code sections, then develop your search using advanced search options such as phrase searching.

D. Updating Statutes

As mentioned in Chapter 2, a researcher should never rely on a source without confirming that it is still "good law." As applied to statutes, this principle means that a researcher must verify that a particular statute is still in force and has not been amended, repealed, superseded by subsequent legislation, or struck down by a case.

State and federal statutes can be updated using KeyCite on Westlaw or Shepard's on Lexis. Bloomberg's citator service, BCite, does not currently cover statutes. Because statutes differ from cases in how they are created and updated, the results retrieved from KeyCite and Shepard's when updating statutes are different from those retrieved when updating cases. Fortunately, the process of updating statutes is much like the process of updating cases, which is discussed fully in Chapter 8.

When viewing a statutory section on Westlaw, KeyCite tabs will be displayed across the top of the document. On Lexis, click on the "Shepardize this document" link to view the citing sources. Next, view the listed citing sources and examine any accompanying symbols. If necessary, restrict the search. The final and most important step is to carefully examine the citing sources to determine whether and how they affect the statute. The information retrieved from Westlaw and Lexis differs slightly, as the following sections explain.

1. Using KeyCite on Westlaw

KeyCite information is integrated into each document on Westlaw. With regard to statutes specifically, KeyCite tabs displayed at the top of the selected code section provide quick access to citing references, negative treatment, and other information related to that section. The "Citing References" tab list includes links to cases and secondary sources, such as *American Law Reports*, *Strong's North Carolina Index*, and law review and journal articles citing that section of the code. The "History" tab provides a summary of how the section has changed over time, links to prior versions of the section, and legislative history documents when available. The "Context and Analysis" tab provides references to other relevant statutes, regulations, and secondary sources selected by West editors.

KeyCite uses a set of flags and symbols to represent the editors' opinion of the validity of a code section. A red flag means the section may have been amended, ruled unconstitutional, superseded, or repealed. A yellow flag means a section may have been renumbered or moved within the code, or a court may have questioned the section or decided that the section is constitutionally limited in some aspect. Another possibility is that some proposed legislation or a recently enacted session law may affect the statute.

2. Using Shepard's on Lexis

To Shepardize a statutory section, click on the "Shepardize this document" link on the code section page displayed to access the Shepard's report. Shepard's assigns a symbol to each statutory section that serves as a quick guide to the current legal status of that section. A red exclamation point suggests that legislative or judicial changes affect the section. A yellow exclamation point suggests that pending legislation may affect the statute.

Shepard's for statutes is broken down into three parts: History, Citing Decisions, and Other Citing Sources. The screen defaults to the "Citing Decisions" tab, which provides a list of cases that have cited to the statutory section you are researching. The "Other Citing Sources" tab provides a list of all law review and journal articles, treatises, annotated statutes, court documents, Restatements, and other secondary source documents on Lexis that cite your statutory section. The "History" tab lists the session laws that created or amended the code section.

3. Restricting Statutory Updates

A useful feature when using either KeyCite or Shepard's is the ability to enter the narrowest section of the relevant code to retrieve the most focused citation information with the least amount of irrelevant information. Alternatively, to receive broader, more comprehensive results, you should use a citation higher in the statutory hierarchy, for example a citation for the part or subchapter above the relevant section. The need to expand your results may initially be difficult to determine. It may be safer to retrieve a broader, more comprehensive citation report and then limit the results as necessary.

Lexis's *Subsection Reports* is an excellent tool for locating citing references for specific sections of the code. Researchers can see the cases that cite specifically to a portion of the statute they are researching by clicking the "Subsection reports by specific court citation" link located at the top of the Shepard's report. This gives a list of the cases that have cited to the selected subsection.

III. Tools for the Toolbox

Constitutions

1. Use annotated versions of the state or federal code to access the North Carolina and United States Constitutions.
2. Free versions of the constitutions are available at the North Carolina General Assembly website and the U.S. Government Publishing Office website respectively.

Statutes

1. Use annotated versions of the state or federal code (print or online) for the best results when searching for relevant statutory law.
   a. North Carolina—*General Statutes of North Carolina Annotated or West's North Carolina General Statutes Annotated*
   b. Federal—*United States Code Annotated* (U.S.C.A.) or *United States Code Service* (U.S.C.S.)
2. The index is the most efficient method for locating statutes in the code.
3. Always use a citator such as Shepard's or KeyCite to ensure the statute you are relying on is good law.

Chapter Five

Legislative History Research and Bill Tracking

I. Introduction

When a statute governs your research question, finding that statute is critically important. Chapter 4 described the process of finding statutes. Equally important, however, is understanding what the statute means. This process is called *statutory construction.*

Statutory construction always begins with the plain language of the statute. Where the language of a statute is clear and unambiguous, the statute must be construed according to its plain meaning.

When the language of a statute is ambiguous, lawyers have many tools at their disposal to help them understand the statute's meaning. When using any of these tools, remember that the primary goal of statutory construction is to ascertain the meaning that is most consistent with the legislature's purpose in enacting the statute.

One tool of statutory construction is the definitions section of a statute, if there is one. However, many statutes do not have definitions sections. Moreover, even when a statute has a definitions section, the definitions themselves may need interpreting.

Another tool of statutory construction is the *canons of construction*—well-established rules that guide lawyers and judges in their examination of statutory language. For example, the canon *expressio unius est exclusio alterius* ("the expression of one thing is the exclusion of another") posits that when a statute expressly mentions one or more items of a class, it impliedly excludes all other items of the same class that are not mentioned.[1]

1. See the Legal Information Institute website's Wex legal dictionary for more information on statutory construction: law.cornell.edu/wex/statutory_construction.

When these intrinsic tools of statutory construction do not lead to a reasonable interpretation of a statute, lawyers and judges must look to extrinsic tools of statutory construction. The two most common extrinsic tools are *legislative history* and *judicial opinions*. This chapter describes the process of researching a statute's legislative history; Chapter 8 describes the process of researching judicial opinions (cases).

To conduct effective legislative history research, whether you are working with a North Carolina statute or a federal statute, you must first understand how statutes are drafted and enacted. While the legislative process in North Carolina is similar to the federal legislative process, there are some important differences. One is the volume of materials produced; while there are often vast amounts of legislative history materials generated and published at the federal level, the generation and publication of state legislative materials varies widely. Many states produce and publish little to no documentation of the legislative process, and the documentation that is published has traditionally been difficult to access. North Carolina is no exception. Fortunately, the development of online resources has greatly improved access to the documents generated in the legislative process in North Carolina.

This chapter (1) discusses the structure of the North Carolina legislative branch and describes the steps in the state's legislative process; (2) introduces tools for tracking current legislation; (3) explains the steps required to research legislative history in North Carolina; and (4) describes the federal legislative process and introduces online resources for federal legislative history research.

II. North Carolina Legislative Research

As noted in prior chapters, North Carolina is one of forty-nine states with a bicameral legislature.[2] North Carolina's legislative body is called the General Assembly, and it consists of two chambers: the House of Representatives and the Senate. The House is composed of 120 members, and the Senate is composed of fifty members. All members of both chambers are elected for two-year terms each even-numbered year. Each chamber does much of its work in committees made up of legislators. Members are supported in their legislative work by a staff of non-legislators.

---

2. Nebraska is the only state with a unicameral legislature. Members of the Nebraska legislature are called Senators. See the Nebraska Legislature Website: nebraskalegislature.gov/education/lesson3.php.

Each General Assembly meets for a two-year session. The first (or long) session of a General Assembly begins in January of each odd-numbered year. The second (or short) session of a General Assembly convenes each even-numbered year. Later that same year, new statewide elections are held to elect senators and representatives for the next General Assembly.

All bills introduced in the General Assembly follow a specific process according to detailed rules of legislative procedure. At each stage of the process, specific types of documentation may be produced. Table 5-1 describes legislative actions and the corresponding documentation that is produced at each stage of the process.

A. Tracking Current North Carolina Legislation

Suppose you are an attorney working for a corporation located in North Carolina. You will need to be aware of pending legislation that may impact the corporation's business interests. *Bill tracking* is the process of following or "tracking" the progress of pending legislation. Researchers tracking current legislation in North Carolina must become familiar with the state-specific online resources for bill tracking. Many states, including North Carolina, have sophisticated legislative websites, and researchers will find a wealth of information on these free sites. Commercial platforms also provide access to some state legislative documents, most commonly the text of bills and their status information. Locating and tracking current state legislation online is a fairly simple task. Finding interpretive documents (i.e., committee reports) can be quite challenging, however, because very little documentation is published by the North Carolina General Assembly.

1. The General Assembly Website

The North Carolina General Assembly provides free access to current legislative information on its website.[3] The General Assembly's website is very easy to navigate and is an excellent repository of historical state legislative information.

Bill tracking is simplest when you know the bill number. From the General Assembly website's homepage, select the current session and enter the bill number in the "Find a Bill" search box. In addition to the various versions of the bill, the retrieved results will include the current status of the bill, the bill's sponsors, the vote history of the bill, and a running record of all the activity

3. ncleg.gov.

Table 5-1. Documenting the North Carolina Legislative Process

Legislative Action	Documentation of the Process
A citizen, interest group, or legislator may promote an idea for a bill.	
The General Assembly leadership may appoint a committee to investigate the idea and submit a study report, identifying the need for the legislation.	**Study reports**, when available, are an important piece of legislative history of a bill in North Carolina. The reports provide intent and reasons why legislation should be passed.
A bill may be drafted by any competent person. The General Assembly's support agency, the Legislative Services Commission, has a Bill Drafting Division and Research Division that draft bills at the request of members.	The **bill text**, if the bill is adopted, is the actual body of language of the statute. Different versions of the bill as it passes through the legislative process might shed light on legislative intent.
The bill is introduced in either chamber of the General Assembly by a member of that chamber. The Reading Clerk reads the name of the sponsor, the bill number, and the bill title aloud on the floor of the chamber. This is the first reading.	The bill must be placed on the **House** or **Senate calendar** to be introduced.
The bill is assigned to a committee or subcommittee for deliberations.	
If the committee or subcommittee decides to favorably report the bill out of committee, it is returned to the floor of the chamber where a second and third reading take place, possibly with some deliberation.	There is no explanatory report. Committee hearings are recorded, but there are no transcripts. The committee's secretary creates brief **committee minutes** from the recording and files the minutes with the Legislative Library. The recordings are not retained.
That chamber might vote to pass the bill after several more readings. If not, the bill dies. If the chamber passes the bill, it is *engrossed* in that chamber and the bill moves to the second chamber in the General Assembly.	North Carolina does not produce a transcript of floor debate. Instead summaries of daily activities are recorded in the ***House Journals*** and ***Senate Journals***. Final vote tallies are also recorded there. Individual voting records for each bill and legislator for each session are available at the General Assembly website. The "Bill Reports" page at the General Assembly website links to "**House Bills passed in the House**" and "**Senate Bills passed in the Senate.**"
In the second chamber, the bill has its first reading and assignment to committee.	

The second chamber's committee may have a hearing. If the bill is reported out of the committee, it is returned to the floor of the second chamber where a second and third reading take place.	As in the first chamber, there is no explanatory report from the committee. Committee hearing transcripts are not made, although hearings are recorded. The committee's secretary creates brief **committee minutes** from the recording and files the minutes with the Legislative Library. The recordings are not retained.
The second chamber may either vote to pass the bill, pass the bill with amendments, or not pass the bill. Generally, the bill dies if it is not passed. If the bill is passed with amendments, then the bill is returned to the first chamber, which will either concur in the amendments or reject them.	North Carolina does not produce a transcript of floor debate. The best record of floor action is the summaries of daily activities recorded in the ***House Journals*** and ***Senate Journals***. Final vote tallies are also recorded there. Individual voting records for each bill and legislator for each session are available at the General Assembly website. The "Bill Reports" page also links to "**House Bills passed in the Senate**" and "**Senate Bills passed in the House.**"
If the first chamber rejects the amendments from the second chamber, a conference committee is created composed of members of both chambers to resolve the differences. If the differences are not resolved, the bill dies.	If the second chamber passes the bill, or the bill is passed by the conference committee, then both chambers must pass the final bill. The bill is now *enrolled*. **Enrolled bills** are available from the General Assembly website by bill number.
The enrolled bill is then signed by the presiding officer of each chamber and becomes a *ratified bill*.	**Ratified bills** are available from the General Assembly website by bill number.
Ratified bills are referred to the Governor for his or her signature. (In North Carolina, however, a small number of ratified bills become law without the Governor's signature.)	A list of "**Ratified Bills Pending on the Governor's desk**" is available at the website.
If the Governor signs the bill, it becomes law. If the Governor fails to act on the bill within 10 days while the General Assembly is in session, the bill becomes law. The Governor may veto the bill.	Bills signed by the Governor are identified as "**Chaptered Bills**" on the General Assembly website. A chart of "**Vetoed Bills**" is also available at the site.
If the Governor vetoes the bill, the bill is returned to the original chamber where three-fifths of those members present and voting may override the veto. If so, the bill is sent to the second chamber where three-fifths of those members present and voting may also vote to override the veto. If the override vote is successful, the bill becomes law. If not, the bill dies.	
After the bill becomes law, it is given a chapter number and is published as part of the North Carolina Session Laws for that General Assembly session.	

related to the bill since it was first introduced. The information is usually updated within a day or two during the legislative session. The website has bill reports, with bill tracking information, for bills beginning with the 1985 General Assembly session.

If you do not know the bill number, the General Assembly website allows you to perform a simple bill text search by first selecting the session and then entering relevant keywords you expect to appear in the text of the bill or in the bill title. This search will generate a set of bills accompanied by the same detailed current status information described above.

Alternatively, you can open the "Legislation/Bills Page" from the Legislation/Bills tab on the website's homepage.[4] From there, you can search for bills in various ways, including browsing the current status of bills at the "Bill Reports" page.[5] You can narrow your search according to the following categories: bills with actions in the current session, House bills passed in the House, House bills passed in the Senate, Senate bills passed in the House, Senate bills passed in the Senate, bills in conference, bills to be ratified, and chaptered bills by bill number. The General Assembly "Bill Reports" page also links to a list of ratified bills currently pending on the Governor's desk and a list of bills already signed by the Governor.

2. Other Online Sources for Tracking North Carolina Legislation

Although the free General Assembly website provides the most convenient and current tools for bill tracking, there are other sources of bill tracking information. Both Westlaw and Lexis offer limited options for North Carolina bill tracking.

Westlaw's "North Carolina Bill Tracking" database provides summaries and status information for legislation from the current or most recently ended legislative session. Bills are tracked from their introduction throughout the legislative process, and information is updated daily. Bill tracking information from previous General Assembly sessions is available back to 2005 in a separate Westlaw database called "North Carolina Bill Tracking: Historical."

In Lexis, the "North Carolina Statutes & Legislation" page includes the "North Carolina Bill Tracking Reports" database. This database contains a summary and legislative chronology of pending bills from the current legislative session; information is updated Monday through Saturday during the peak of the legislative session and Monday through Friday at all other times. The "NC

4. ncleg.gov/Legislation/Legislation.html.
5. ncleg.gov/Legislation/BillReports.html.

Full-Text Bills" database includes the text of bills pending in the current legislative session as well as retrospective coverage back to 1993. The "North Carolina Legislative Bill History" database includes selected Fiscal Notes and Governor's Messages for legislation from 2006 to the current legislative session and limited coverage back to 2002.

The North Carolina Bar Association (NCBA) maintains its own Legislative Tracking System, a free online tool hosted on the NCBA website and powered by Congressional Quarterly's CQ Roll Call.[6]

3. Other Options for Tracking Current North Carolina Legislation

In addition to the options listed above, any interested person can get information about the status of current legislation from the Bill Status (Video) System by contacting the Bill Status Desk in the Legislative Library by telephone at (919) 733-7779 or in person in Room 2226 of the State Legislative Building.

Also, UNC-TV produces a weekly public affairs television show called *Legislative Week in Review*.[7] The show includes reporting on issues related to legislative activities in the North Carolina General Assembly as well as interviews with lawmakers. The show also highlights pending legislation and reviews the week's legislative events. The UNC-TV website features additional information and streaming video from the show. Video archives are also available.

Finally, the University of North Carolina School of Government has established a reputation for excellent reporting on North Carolina legislative activities. Since 1935, the School of Government's Legislative Reporting Service (LRS) has prepared neutral, nonpartisan legislative summaries. Beginning in 2019, the LRS digest of bills and legislative actions for each legislative day is available for free on the UNC School of Government website and the General Assembly website.[8] The School of Government's website includes all of the digests and the following additional tools for legislative research: *The Daily Bulletin*, a compilation of the digests for each legislative day; *My Bills*, a "folder" where users may store all bills of interest to their research; and *My Monitors*, a tool that allows users to keep track of bills that include proposed changes in subject areas of interest.

6. ncbar.org/members/governmental-affairs/bill-tracking.
7. video.unctv.org/show/north-carolina-now-legislative-week-review.
8. lrs.sog.unc.edu; ncleg.gov.

B. Researching North Carolina Legislative History

Of course, not all legislative history research involves bill tracking. In fact, the majority of legislative history research grows out of the need to interpret a provision of a statute (a bill that has already been enacted). This section of this chapter explains the process of researching the legislative history of a statute, as outlined in Table 5-2.

Table 5-2. Process of Legislative History Research in North Carolina

Step 1	Identify the session law numbers.
Step 2	Read the session law text.
Step 3	Review the bill chronology and earlier versions of the bill on the North Carolina General Assembly website. For pre-1985 bills, create the chronology of legislative actions from the *House* and *Senate Journals*.
Step 4	Review committee minutes.
Step 5	Review notes from floor debate or actions in the House and Senate Journals.
Step 6	Read any legislative study reports that are available.
Step 7	Read the Governor's signing statement or reported comments if available.

1. Methods of Researching Legislative History/ Types of Legislative History

a. Identify the Session Law Number

In North Carolina, both codifications of state statutes, the *General Statutes of North Carolina Annotated* and *West's North Carolina General Statutes Annotated,* as well as the free version of the General Statutes on the General Assembly website, provide references to the session laws that added and amended the statutory provisions. These references are labeled as "history" and appear just after the statutory text in all versions. When researching statutes on Westlaw, it is important to note that statutes enacted before 1943 have no "history" notes, so you must consult another source to obtain session law information.

b. Read the Session Law Text

To locate the text of a session law, locate the session law number at the end of the statute that codified the session law. For example, "(1983, c. 701, s. 1.)" refers to section 1 of chapter 701 of the 1983 *Session Laws,* and "(2005-344, s. 1)" refers to section 1 of chapter 344 of the 2005 *Session Laws.* Using this session law number, locate the text of the original session law as passed by the General

Assembly and the text of any session laws making subsequent amendments to the statute. Refer to Chapter 4 for specific instructions on finding North Carolina session laws.

Read the session law text to identify or confirm which parts of the session law are relevant to the legal question you are researching. Remember that a single code section can be the end result of many session laws. To do thorough legislative history research, you must determine which session laws enacted or changed the specific part of the code section at issue.

c. Review the Final Bill and Previous Versions

The text of each session law also includes the bill number for the House or Senate bill that eventually became that session law. Using this bill number, you can go to the North Carolina General Assembly website[9] and retrieve the bill. The "Find Bills by Number" search box on the homepage retrieves bills for each General Assembly session going back to 1985. The associated bill report is simply a chronological history of the bill as it traveled through the legislative process, not an actual statement about the intent behind the legislation. The report may contain links to earlier versions of the bill; the various versions of the bill that were rejected or amended during the process may shed light on the legislative intent behind the bill. While there may not be convenient hypertext links to other related documentation (e.g., committee minutes, the names of the committees involved, and date the bill was reported out of committee), the information in the report can be useful in locating these additional documents.

d. Use Journals for Pre-1985 Bill Reports

For pre-1985 bills, researchers attempting to locate legislative history information must consult the *North Carolina House Journal* and *Senate Journal.* A bill number index includes references to the journal page numbers where you can find information about actions taken on each bill. The State Library of North Carolina makes the *Journals* available online from 1822 to present.[10] Academic law libraries and many state government libraries have print copies of the *North Carolina House Journal* and *Senate Journal.*

e. Review the Committee Minutes

From the bill chronology or report, identify the name(s) of the committee(s) that deliberated about the bill. Brief committee meeting minutes might be

---

9. ncleg.gov.
10. ncgovdocs.org.

available at the Legislative Library in Raleigh. The minutes might also include staff member notes or background reports. Minutes of standing committees are available from 1967 to the present.

Minutes of specially appointed non-standing and study committees are also available from 1963 to the present. As minutes are microfilmed or otherwise reformatted, these collections shift, and the dates of coverage may change. To that end, some minutes may be unavailable for periods of time as they are reformatted.[11]

f. Floor Debate

The General Assembly provides links to live floor debate in both the Senate and the House. These links can be accessed from the General Assembly website's homepage. The House floor debates for the current session are audio recorded and archived on the website and can be accessed from the House page.[12] The Senate also audio-records its daily floor debates, but the recordings are not currently available on the website. Rather, the audiotapes are transferred to the State Archives, where they can be accessed at the end of the biennial session. Although the General Assembly does not provide verbatim written transcripts of floor debates, summaries of floor actions are recorded in the *House* and *Senate Journals*.

g. Study Reports

The General Assembly leadership or the Governor may appoint ad hoc study committees or commissions. A standing committee of the General Assembly might also be directed to study an issue. Once information is collected, a study report is issued.[13] A study report might explain the need for specific legislation and give the General Assembly guidance in legislatively addressing an issue. The report might also include findings, recommendations, and perhaps even a proposed bill draft. Therefore, the study report can provide some context for understanding legislative intent.

---

11. For more precise information about the contents and availability of these materials, visit the legislative library website: ncleg.gov/library/LegHistMaterials/leghist materials.html.

12. ncleg.gov/House.

13. North Carolina study reports are similar to United States congressional committee prints at the federal level. In addition to the factual findings, North Carolina study reports may include more recommendations than federal committee prints.

Many study reports are available online, though there is no central repository for them. Selected study reports are digitized by the Legislative Library and are available on the General Assembly website accessible from the "Legislative Publications" page (via the Divisions dropdown menu on the home page).[14] Coverage includes selected study reports from 1927 to the present. The Legislative Library's website[15] provides the same set of study reports in a convenient list of titles arranged both by year and by subject. The list also provides library call numbers for print copies of selected study reports that are available for viewing at the Legislative Library in Raleigh. A select few other libraries, including the North Carolina Supreme Court Library may have a small collection of study reports.

Several agencies of the General Assembly, such as the Legislative Research Commission and the General Statutes Commission, also may make recommendations for specific legislation. A collection of reports or minutes from these commissions is available at the Legislative Library.

h. Governor's Statements

Governor's statements concerning North Carolina legislation are not very common and are difficult to locate.[16] The Governor's website provides access to written press releases and audio/video releases that occasionally relate to legislation. The Governor's public statements about legislation might also be recorded by local media, such as the Raleigh *News and Observer* newspaper.[17]

Eventually, a North Carolina Governor's public papers and statements will be published by the North Carolina Department of Cultural Resources; however, there is a significant delay in the publication of these materials, and they are not widely available.

The Governor of North Carolina was granted veto power in 1997. Vetoes and veto statements transmitted to the General Assembly are noted in the bill tracking reports on the General Assembly's website; the reports include a link to the full text of written veto statements. A chart of North Carolina's veto history and statistics can be found online.[18]

---

14. ncleg.gov.

15. ncleg.gov/library/Collections/studies/year.html.

16. In contrast, presidential signing statements are readily available at the federal level.

17. newsobserver.com.

18. ncleg.gov/library/Documents/VetoStats.pdf.

2. Westlaw and Lexis as Sources of State Legislative History

Westlaw and Lexis provide less precise options for researching North Carolina legislative history. Westlaw provides a database, "North Carolina Legislative History," which includes the following sections:

- Bill Summaries from the 2000 Regular Session of the 1999 General Assembly through the 2008 Regular Session of the 2008 General Assembly.
- Governor's Messages from 2000 through the current session.
- House Journals from the 2001 General Assembly (2001–2002) through July 28, 2006 of the 2006 Second Session of the 2005 General Assembly and from the 2011 General Assembly through the 2015 Regular Session of the 2015 General Assembly.
- Senate Journals from the 2001 General Assembly (2001–2002) through the 2003 Regular Session of the 2003 General Assembly and from the 2011 General Assembly through the 2015 Regular Session of the 2015 General Assembly.
- House vote transcripts from the 2001 General Assembly through current sessions.

Lexis includes a "North Carolina Legislative Bill History" database. Selective coverage begins in 2002, and the document types included in the database are "Governor's Messages" and "Fiscal Notes."

3. Uniform Laws and Model Acts

At the state level, it is important to be aware of the source of the statute you are researching. Many state statutes are patterned after uniform laws or model acts. You may be familiar with uniform laws and model acts from your law school courses. Examples include the Uniform Commercial Code (UCC) and the Model Penal Code (MPC). Uniform laws and model acts aim to unify statutory law across jurisdictional boundaries and provide a more standardized, rational replacement for common law.

Many organizations participate in drafting uniform laws and model acts, but the vast majority are initially drafted by the Uniform Law Commission (ULC), formerly known as the National Conference of Commissioners on Uniform State Laws. The ULC website provides the text of all uniform laws created by the ULC as well as helpful maps and information on state adoption of individual uniform laws and model acts.[19] Sometimes states pass uniform laws

---

19. uniformlaws.org.

and model acts as written; other times, they adopt versions that include their own changes. Uniform laws and model acts, as well as information about their adoption, can also be found in the *Uniform Laws Annotated* on Westlaw and in the print version published by Thomson Reuters.

If the source of a state statute is a uniform law or model act, your research will generally be much easier because you will have access to legislative histories from other states as well as analysis and commentary in law reviews and other secondary sources. According to the ULC, uniform laws attempt to bring "clarity and stability to critical areas of state statutory law."[20] Thus, uniform laws and model acts have become popular subjects for articles by legal scholars, and these articles usually analyze the differences between state statutes.

III. Researching Federal Legislative History

A North Carolina practitioner sometimes encounters issues of federal law that may require researching the legislative history of federal statutes. While this process is similar to the process of researching the legislative history of state statutes, it is often easier, because researchers have abundant digital access to federal legislative information. From free government websites that provide digitally signed PDF versions of legislative documents to commercial databases that offer vast historical collections and compiled legislative histories, researchers benefit from a treasure trove of electronic resources that make federal legislative research significantly easier than it was when these documents existed only in print or microform.

A. Summary of the Federal Legislative Process

The process of enacting a federal statute begins with the introduction of a bill in one of the chambers of the United States Congress, either the House of Representatives or the Senate. The bill is assigned to a committee where deliberations may occur. While a bill is in committee, committee staff may prepare a committee print comprising research, documentation, and other information about the subject of the bill. If hearings are held, transcripts of testimony and statements are created. The committee might submit a report reviewing in detail the elements of the bill, the need for the legislation, and a recommendation for passage. Committee reports are usually the most important statements of legislative intent.

---

20. uniformlaws.org/aboutulc/overview.

If a bill is reported favorably by committee, it moves to the floor of each chamber for floor debate. Floor debate is transcribed and published in the *Congressional Record*. If the bill is passed by the first chamber, it moves to the second chamber, where the process is repeated. If the second chamber approves the bill in the same form as in the first chamber, the bill is enrolled and sent to the President for signature. If the bill is passed in the second chamber with amendments, however, a conference committee must be created to attempt to negotiate the differences. If the conference committee reaches agreement, then the bill is returned to both chambers to be approved and thereafter sent to the President for signature.

When presented with a bill passed by Congress, the President may sign the bill into law, ignore the bill (in which case it may become law anyway, depending upon the timing of the legislative session), or veto the bill. If the President signs the bill into law, it becomes a *public law* and is assigned a public law number. For example, Pub. L. 111-148 refers to the 148th public law passed in the 111th Congress. Public laws are often referred to by popular name. The popular name can be included in the name of the public law itself, such as the "The Patient Protection and Affordable Care Act," or can arise through common usage, such as "Obamacare."

A new public law is first published as a *slip law*. At the end of each legislative session, the public laws enacted in that session are compiled and published in chronological order in the *United States Statutes at Large*. Eventually, the Law Revision Council of the United States House of Representatives codifies each new public law in the *United States Code*. See Table 5-3 for a comparison of North Carolina and federal legislative actions.

B. Tracking Current United States Legislation

1. Congress.gov

Tracking the status of federal legislation currently pending in Congress is a common research task, and researchers benefit from free online access to current and archived federal legislative information. The Library of Congress and the United States Government Publishing Office (GPO) provide free public access to official legislative publications.

The Library of Congress created the Congress.gov website to provide free access to current and archived legislative information. Congress.gov provides access to bill status reports that contain an up-to-date running list of activity concerning each bill. Because so much federal legislative history is available online, the status reports often link directly to the full text of related documents,

Table 5-3. Comparison of Sources for North Carolina and Federal Legislative History

Action	North Carolina Sources	Federal Sources
Pre-Legislative Action	**Study reports** may be produced by ad hoc or standing legislative committees. The reports determine the need for legislation and make recommendations. Reports may be an important source of legislative intent.	
Introduction of Bills	**Bills** are introduced by legislators and published at the General Assembly website (ncga.state.nc.us).	**Bills** are introduced by legislators and published at the Government Publishing Office's website (govinfo.gov).
Committee Work	**Minutes** of committee meetings and perhaps exhibits or notes are filed with the Legislative Library. Committees also file less useful form reports, containing only simple recommendations.	**Committee prints** (documentation of related information by committee staffers). **Committee hearings** (transcripts of witness testimony and other statements). **Committee reports** (the most persuasive piece of legislative history).
Floor Debate	***House Journal*** records a summary of daily activity and is published at the end of the session. ***Senate Journal*** records a summary of daily activity and is published at the end of the session.	**Congressional Record** publishes the recorded debates on the floor of the U.S. House and Senate each day.
Session Laws	***North Carolina Session Laws***	***Statutes at Large***
Codified Law	***General Statutes of North Carolina (official)*** ***West's North Carolina General Statutes Annotated*** ***General Statutes of North Carolina (on the General Assembly website)***	***United States Code (official)*** ***United States Code Annotated*** ***United States Code Service***

such as committee reports, floor debates published in the *Congressional Record*, amendments, and recorded votes. Using the bill reports from Congress.gov is the best method of tracking current federal legislation.

The Congress.gov homepage includes a search box for locating bill status by bill number or key words. The search results list leads to summaries for each bill, as well as the sponsor, the date of introduction, the latest action taken on the bill, any committee reports, and votes. Selecting one of the tabs along the bottom of the result screen provides more details. The "Summary" tab provides a short explanation of each version of the bill. The "Text" tab displays the text of the most recent version of the bill and also allows you to select a different version of the bill or click on a link to a PDF that is certified by the United States Superintendent of Documents as an official version of the bill. The "Actions" tab lists all actions taken on the bill but can be filtered to list only major actions. The "Amendments" tab includes proposed changes offered during the legislative process. The "Cosponsors" tab includes every member of Congress who has agreed to sponsor the legislation and the date of each sponsorship. The "Committees" tab lists all committees associated with the bill and their activity, including committee reports. The "Related Bills" tab includes bills identified by Congress or its staff as similar in subject or related procedurally during the same two-year congressional term.

A service of the GPO, Govinfo.gov provides free access to official publications from all three branches of the federal government. Govinfo.gov is an excellent repository of federal government documents, and the site provides several helpful search options for researching legislative information. Keyword and advanced search options are available. You may also choose to search by date, subject area, committee, or author. Govinfo.gov does not include a legislative bill report feature.

2. Other Online Sources for Tracking Federal Legislation

Although Congress.gov is the best source for tracking bills enacted into law since 1995, there are other free and commercial options.

a. GovTrack.us

GovTrack.us is an independent website that publishes the status of federal legislation and information about members of Congress, including voting records, and original research on bills and votes. GovTrack.us allows users to receive email alerts on congressional actions related to a bill and to track actions of a member of Congress or the activity of a particular committee. Users can track documents that have particular combinations of words, relate to an individual bill number, or affect a *United States Code* section.

b. Commercial Options

Westlaw, Lexis, and Bloomberg all have tools for tracking federal legislation. Westlaw's "Federal Bill Tracking" database includes summaries and status information for pending legislation in the current session of the United States Congress. The "Bill Tracking: Historical" database provides summaries and status information for legislation introduced in past congressional sessions starting with 2005. Email alerts are available in both versions. Lexis includes bill tracking information in the "Congressional Bill Tracking Reports" database. Reports for the current session of Congress are updated daily, and users can set up email alerts. Historical bill tracking reports are available for previous sessions of Congress back to 1989. On Bloomberg, bills from the current Congress are available in the "Legislative Resources" tab, and users can set up alerts for activity on current legislation. Bills from previous Congresses are available back to 1993 in the "Congressional Bill Search" database.

Two other popular commercial sources for federal bill tracking and legislative history are ProQuest Congressional and ProQuest Legislative Insight. These platforms are powerful tools that have the most comprehensive collection of federal legislative documents. While they are generally accessible only through academic libraries (including law school libraries), you may wish to use these platforms when having a complete collection of legislative history documents is important to your legal research and you cannot find an already compiled legislative history.

C. Federal Legislative History Shortcuts

In contrast to state legislatures, the United States Congress produces abundant documentation of the federal legislative process. Fortunately, there are several shortcuts available to help researchers navigate this wealth of information.

1. Annotated Codes

Westlaw maintains a *United States Code Annotated* (U.S.C.A.) database in which you can find references, and sometimes links, to the full text of relevant legislative history documents. For a particular code section, select the "History" tab. The Editor's and Revisor's Notes section of the tab provides a short summary of the changes to the section made by each session law, allowing you to select which session law is relevant. The Legislative History section of the tab provides a list of documents available on Westlaw for each session law that has affected your code section. Currently, Lexis does not integrate legislative history documents into its online or print versions of the United States Code.

2. Compiled Histories

The most important shortcut when researching federal legislative history is to use a commercially prepared *compiled legislative history*. Several publishers compile and publish complete legislative histories that include all legislative documents related to a specific public law. Law libraries collect these compiled legislative histories, and they are usually well indexed. Although there are no free online collections of compiled legislative histories, Westlaw, Lexis, and HeinOnline are gradually adding compiled legislative histories for major public laws to their online collections in individual databases. For example, Westlaw has a large collection of compiled legislative histories on a variety of topics in the "U.S. GAO Federal Legislative Histories" database.

3. Committee Reports

If a compiled legislative history is not available, focus on finding the committee report, which is widely viewed as the most important piece of legislative history. Committee reports are readily available on Congress.gov back to 1995. Selected reports are available back to the 1940s on Westlaw and 1990 on Lexis.

4. Collecting Your Own Legislative History

As with state legislative history research, collecting the legislative history of a federal public law is a time-consuming task. It is made easier, however, by the superior documentation of the process and the online availability of the various types of documents.

Similar to the process in North Carolina, it is usually easiest to work backwards to collect federal legislative history documents. The best starting point at the federal level is a statute, preferably from an annotated code. Immediately after the text of the statute in the annotated code, you will find legislative history notes that will include both the *Statutes at Large* citation and the public law number for the legislation that affected the statute you are researching. In the editor's notes, you may find an explanation of how each session law changed the text of the statute. This can help you determine which session laws affected the portion of the text you are concerned with. Alternatively, you may find the same information by using the Popular Name Table index in any of the *United States Code* versions, where the popular names of public laws are arranged alphabetically. Beside each popular name is the U.S.C. citation as well as citations to the public law numbers and *Statutes at Large* citations for legislation affecting the statute you are researching. Working either online or in print, you can use these citations to find specific related documents. For example, you can enter these citations in Congress.gov to retrieve recent committee reports or pages from the *Congressional Record* covering floor debate.

IV. Tools for the Toolbox

1. Use the North Carolina General Assembly website to track current state legislative action as well as archived legislative information.
2. Bill tracking sites are available for free online for both state and federal legislation.
3. The most efficient approach to legislative history research starts with the finished product—the statute.
4. Compiled legislative histories are available online and in print for many federal statutes and are excellent timesavers.
5. Annotated codes include historical information and provide a shortcut for legislative history research.

Chapter Six

Administrative Law

When your research question involves the application of a statute, whether state or federal, your research is not complete until you determine whether there are any relevant *regulations* or other administrative decisions that accompany your statute. Administrative law—the decisions and rules (regulations) of administrative agencies—is primary law, like statutes and cases. However, new researchers are often less familiar with administrative law than with other kinds of primary law. This chapter begins with an introduction to administrative law and how it is created, followed by a description of the techniques and available tools for researching North Carolina administrative law and federal administrative law.

I. Administrative Agencies Generally

Administrative law is promulgated by administrative agencies created by state and federal governments to provide expertise in various specialized areas of the law.[1] These administrative agencies fall under the executive branch of the state and federal governments and are subject to the ultimate authority of the chief executive—the Governor of North Carolina or the President of the United States.

Significantly, administrative agencies have quasi-legislative power, including the power to issue *regulations* that implement and interpret legislative and executive mandates. They also have quasi-executive power, including the power

1. Note that the head of the executive branch, the governor (state government) or President (federal government), may issue new orders and proclamations on his or her own authority, pardon individuals, reorganize executive departments, and make appointments, among other powers. The documents created through the exercise of these powers have among the same effect as documents issued from administrative agencies, i.e., they are primary authority.

to issue licenses, investigate whether rules are being followed, and enforce rules. Finally, agencies have quasi-judicial power, including the power to adjudicate cases involving disputes between the agencies and citizens. Thus, administrative law spans all three branches of government, making it an important facet of legal research in many instances.

Although administrative agencies span all three branches, their function is nonetheless narrowly tailored to accomplish only particular tasks. Legislative acts granting authority to a particular agency, called *enabling statutes,* prohibit the agency from acting outside of the statutory boundaries put in place when the agency was formed. For example, an administrative rule is invalid if it exceeds the agency's rule-making authority.

Administrative law tends to be highly specialized and may often encompass very complex topics. Nonetheless, administrative law directly affects the lives of citizens in specific and wide-ranging ways. For example, in North Carolina, there are administrative rules detailing when and how crime victims can be compensated[2] and specifying the process for becoming a licensed adult care home.[3] At the federal level, regulations govern subjects as complex as procedures for homeland security[4] and as simple as the warnings required on each cigarette package.[5]

II. North Carolina Administrative Law

Initially, administrative law developed without a uniform structure, process, or publication pattern. In the mid-1940s, after decades of federal and state agencies drafting their own regulations and providing limited public access to them, the federal government created the first federal Administrative Procedures Act addressing this issue at the federal level. The development was slower at the state level, with most states following a similar pattern and eventually adopting a version of the Model State Administrative Procedures Act. North Carolina's Administrative Procedures Act (APA) was first enacted in the 1970s and has been substantially amended several times.[6] The APA defines the process

2. 14B N.C.A.C. 09.0301 et seq. (also found in N.C. Gen. Stat. § 15B-1 et seq. (2017)).

3. 10A N.C.A.C. 13F .0201 et seq. (also found in N.C. Gen. Stat. § 131D-4.1 et seq.) (2018).

4. *See e.g.*, 6 C.F.R. § 3.1 et seq. (2018) (Aliens & Nationality); 8 C.F.R. § 1.1 et seq. (2018) (Domestic Security).

5. 19 C.F.R. § 11.3 (2018).

6. N.C. Gen. Stat. § 150B (2017).

by which administrative rules are created, sets out the procedures to be followed in administrative hearings, and regulates how administrative information is organized and published.

A. Rules

In North Carolina, a *rule* is "any agency regulation, standard, or statement of general applicability that implements or interprets an enactment of the General Assembly or Congress."[7] Rules that (1) are created within the scope of this statutory mandate and (2) follow the process prescribed by the North Carolina APA have the full force and effect of law. Although administrative rules operate like statutes for purposes of legal analysis, if there is a conflict between a statute and an administrative rule, the statute controls.

1. How Administrative Rules Are Created in North Carolina

According to the North Carolina APA, a North Carolina agency proposing a new rule must publish the text of the proposed rule, along with a short reason or explanation for the rule, in a biweekly publication, the *North Carolina Register*. The public is then invited to comment within a specified time period, usually at least sixty days. The agency may also hold a public hearing to receive additional information. Thereafter, the agency considers the public comment(s) and then may adopt the rule. If the adopted rule differs substantially from the originally proposed rule, the rule must be published again in the *North Carolina Register* and go through the same process again.

Once the rule is adopted, the agency must keep the comments and other documentation of the rulemaking process on file and provide them to anyone who inquires. The agency files the adopted rule with the North Carolina Rules Review Commission, a statutory agency comprising ten members appointed by the General Assembly. If the Rules Review Commission determines that the rule is within the authority delegated to the agency by the General Assembly and approves the rule, the rule is codified in the *North Carolina Administrative Code* (N.C.A.C.). Each title of the N.C.A.C. is organized by chapter, sometimes with subchapters and sections. For example, in the citation 21 N.C. Admin. Code 14K.0107, 21 is the title, 14 is the chapter, K is the subchapter, and .0107 is the section. References to chapters are usually omitted when identifying specific regulations.

---

7. N.C. Gen. Stat. § 150B-2(8a) (2017).

Emergency rules and temporary rules are adopted under abbreviated processes when an agency determines that adhering to the notice and hearing requirements of the North Carolina APA would be contrary to the public interest and that the immediate adoption of the rule is required.[8] These rules are generally enacted (1) to meet an imminent threat to public safety, health, or welfare; (2) to prevent a loss of federal or state funding; (3) to meet federal or state deadlines; or (4) to protect human health or the environment.

2. Sources of North Carolina Administrative Rules

North Carolina administrative rules can be found primarily in two publications: the *North Carolina Register* and the *North Carolina Administrative Code* (N.C.A.C.).

a. North Carolina Register

The *North Carolina Register*, published twice a month, includes (1) the text of proposed rules; (2) permanent rules approved by the Rules Review Commission; (3) temporary rules entered into the N.C.A.C.; (4) emergency rules entered into the N.C.A.C.; (5) executive orders of the Governor; and (6) an index to published, contested administrative decisions issued by the North Carolina Office of Administrative Hearings.

The *North Carolina Register* is published by Lexis, and the print copy is available by subscription. The North Carolina Office of Administrative Hearings also publishes the *Register* on the Office's website.[9] Coverage extends back to the first volume and issue in 1986, through a collaboration with the State Library of North Carolina and the Kathrine R. Everett Law Library at the University of North Carolina School of Law.

All three major research services maintain online databases to the *Register*. Westlaw includes current and historical *North Carolina Register* databases (identified as *North Carolina Proposed & Adopted Regulations* and *North Carolina Administrative Register-Historical*, respectively). Coverage for *North Carolina Administrative Register-Historical* began in November 2001, while *North Carolina Proposed & Adopted Regulations* goes back two years. Lexis includes a *North Carolina Register* database with coverage beginning in January 1998.

---

8. N.C. Gen. Stat. § 150B-21.1(a)(adopting temporary rules); N.C. Gen. Stat. § 150B-21.1A (2017) (adopting emergency rules).

9. ncoah.com/rules/register.

Bloomberg also provides a database of proposed, final, emergency, temporary, and interim rules, plus regulatory notices from North Carolina back to 2011. The steps used to find the *North Carolina Register* in each of these sources are set out below in Table 6-1.

Table 6-1. Finding *North Carolina Register* on Electronic Sources

Electronic Source	Steps to find the *North Carolina Register*
Westlaw	• Go to the "North Carolina Register" database.
Lexis	• Go to the "Browse Sources" link. • Narrow the jurisdiction to North Carolina using the filters in the left margin. • Browse the titles.
Bloomberg	• Select "All Legal Content" under the "Browse" heading. • Select the "Select Sources by U.S. Jurisdiction" tab. • Narrow the jurisdiction to North Carolina. • Select "N.C. Regulatory and Administrative."

For researchers interested in current awareness of administrative rule activity, the Office of Administrative Hearings maintains an email listserv notifying subscribers of the publication of the latest *Register* on its website.

b. North Carolina Administrative Code

The *North Carolina Administrative Code* (N.C.A.C.) contains the rules from twenty-six agencies and more than fifty occupational licensing boards. It is organized by subject and is regularly updated. The official version of the N.C.A.C. is published by Thomson West and contains thirty titles published in a twenty-volume set. The official version is updated with monthly supplements containing rule updates and an index.

The N.C.A.C. is also published on the North Carolina Office of Administrative Hearings website.[10] Although it is not the official version, this convenient version is free and is updated weekly. It is browsable by title and keyword searchable by title or full text. The N.C.A.C. is also available on Westlaw, Lexis, and Bloomberg. These databases appear to be regularly updated. Westlaw also offers historical databases of previous versions of the N.C.A.C. since 2002. The steps used to find the N.C.A.C. in each of these sources are set out below in Table 6-2.

Table 6-2. Finding *North Carolina Administrative Code* on Electronic Sources

Electronic Source	Steps to find the *North Carolina Administrative Code*
Westlaw	• Enter "North Carolina Regulations" in the universal search bar. • Select the title in the "Looking for this?" pop-up link.
Lexis	• Browse the "Sources" search box. • Enter "North Carolina Administrative Code." • Browse the titles.
Bloomberg	• Enter "North Carolina Administrative Code" in the main search bar.

3. Finding North Carolina Administrative Rules

Finding relevant administrative rules can be difficult for several reasons. First, codifications of administrative rules are typically not well indexed. Second, the complex, detailed, and precise nature of the terminology involved makes selecting search terms difficult, whether you are searching a print index or using search terms in a full-text keyword search. As is the case with some other legal sources, it is often easiest to find administrative rules using a source that does not contain the rules themselves. There are several ways to accomplish this.

10. reports.oah.state.nc.us/ncac.asp.

First, you can obtain a citation from another source, such as a law review or journal article, treatise, or judicial opinion. Even if the source does not provide a citation to the relevant administrative rules, the discussion might provide citations to relevant sections of the North Carolina General Statutes, and the annotations to those code sections might include administrative rule citations. Finally, even if the sources do not provide citations to the administrative rules for which you are searching or to related statutes, the discussion in the sources themselves will likely provide clues about relevant search terms to use in a more direct keyword search, if that becomes necessary.

Second, you can research regulations using citations contained in the authorizing or enabling statutes and in other related statutes. One way to do this is to locate the enabling statute in one of the annotated codes, the *General Statutes of North Carolina Annotated* or *West's North Carolina General Statutes Annotated,* and then skim the annotations to locate citations to relevant administrative rules in the *North Carolina Administrative Code.* Another way is to use the "Table of Authority" found in the N.C.A.C. to direct you to the relevant administrative rules. The "Table of Authority" is currently found in volume 20A of the N.C.A.C. and lists all of the North Carolina General Statutes, federal statutes, federal regulations, and non-statutory authority for specific rules in the N.C.A.C.

Third, you can simply browse through the administrative rules by title. Browsing the N.C.A.C. titles is akin to the title or outline approach to searching statutory codes as discussed in Chapter 4. The N.C.A.C. titles can be viewed in print and are also browsable on the North Carolina Office of Administrative Hearings website and on Westlaw, Lexis, and Bloomberg. This method is most effective when you are familiar with the issue you are researching, especially if you have used the N.C.A.C. to research that issue recently. However, this method carries the risk that you will miss material that is hidden in another title whose name might not suggest its relevance to the subject being researched.

Fourth, you can search for a particular administrative rule using the index to the N.C.A.C. Searching this index might be a useful approach if you are familiar with the terminology used in the rule or with the issuing agency. The cumulative supplements include an updated index incorporating new regulations added to the N.C.A.C. since the main annual index was last published. This index volume is only available in print. The index is not available on the Office of Administrative Hearings website or on Westlaw, Lexis, or Bloomberg.

Finally, you can search for administrative rules online through Westlaw, Lexis, and Bloomberg using keywords. On Westlaw and Lexis, you can search the full text of the N.C.A.C., or selected fields or segments, using keywords. Although the Westlaw and Lexis search engines have some capability to anticipate and search for additional relevant terms beyond the ones you enter, your search is most likely to succeed when you know the precise language used in the text you want to retrieve. While Bloomberg provides full text terms and connector searching, it does not currently support natural language or field or segment searching of the N.C.A.C.

4. Using the *North Carolina Register* to Update Your Research

To update a rule in the annually published N.C.A.C., simply check the citation for the rule in the cumulative supplement. Checking the index in the cumulative supplement may also reveal any new related rules. You can also check each *North Carolina Register* issued since the date of the most recent cumulative supplement for any newly approved rules, new temporary rules, or new emergency rules.

The North Carolina Office of Administrative Hearings posts the most recent edition of the *North Carolina Register* online twice a month.[11] Westlaw provides online access to the text of proposed rules from the current *North Carolina Register* in its "North Carolina Proposed & Adopted Regulations—All" database. Lexis includes new *North Carolina Register* rules in the "NC-North Carolina Register" database within two weeks of publication.

B. Administrative Decisions

1. The Adjudication Process

As a quasi-judicial arm of the government, an administrative agency may be called upon to settle or adjudicate disputes involving agency rules and actions. Like many jurisdictions, North Carolina uses both informal and formal hearings to settle particular administrative law matters. Administrative agencies in North Carolina generally have one or two informal opportunities to settle or adjudicate disputes. Thereafter, an aggrieved citizen may use the formal

11. ncoah.com/rules/register/.

process to settle the dispute by filing a contested case with the Office of Administrative Hearings. An administrative law judge (ALJ), who is independent of the agency, is appointed by the Office of Administrative Hearings to hear the case. After hearing the case, the ALJ issues a hearing decision to both the citizen and the agency. The agency makes the final agency decision but must adopt the ALJ's opinion unless it is contrary to the preponderance of the admissible evidence in the record. Finally, if a citizen chooses, she may appeal the agency decision to Superior Court.

2. Finding Administrative Decisions

Beginning in 1998, most administrative decisions have been published annually as a separate volume of the *North Carolina Administrative Code.* Each annual volume includes the full text of all administrative decisions released for publication in that calendar year. These annual volumes also include all recommended decisions of the ALJ and all final agency decisions submitted to the Office of Administrative Hearings. The decisions in each of these annual volumes are organized by month. Additionally, following each month's decisions, there is a list of decisions reported that month without published opinions, such as cases that were dismissed or decided on summary judgment.

Administrative decisions are also posted online at the Office of Administrative Hearings website.[12] Coverage is browsable but not searchable, and the thoroughness of the coverage depends upon the agency. Only a small number of agency decisions are available on the Office of Administrative Hearings website, and they date only as far back as 2001.

Westlaw includes a "North Carolina Administrative Decisions & Guidance" database with coverage back to 2000. Lexis also includes coverage back to 2000 in the "NC Office of Administrative Hearings Decisions" database. In contrast, Bloomberg provides access to North Carolina administrative decisions from a only small number of agencies. The steps used to find North Carolina Administrative Decisions in each of these sources are set out below in Table 6-3.

12. oah.state.nc.us/hearings/decisions.

Table 6-3. Finding North Carolina Administrative Decisions on Electronic Sources

Electronic Source	Steps to find the *North Carolina Administrative Code*
Westlaw	• Enter "North Carolina Administrative Decisions" in the universal search bar. • Select the "North Carolina Administrative Hearings" database from the pop-up window.
Lexis	• Go to the "Browse Sources" link. • Type "NC Office of Administrative Hearings Decisions" to access the decisions database.
Bloomberg	• Select "All Legal Content" under the "Browse" heading. • Select the "Select Sources by U.S. Jurisdiction" tab. • Narrow the jurisdiction to North Carolina. • Select "N.C. Agencies and Departments."

III. Federal Administrative Law

Federal administrative law is created and functions much like North Carolina administrative law. However, unlike North Carolina administrative "rules," federal administrative rules are referred to as administrative "regulations."[13]

The first federal code of administrative law was published in 1938. The first federal Administrative Procedures Act (APA) was enacted in 1946 requiring agencies to keep the public informed of agency organization, procedures, and regulations. The APA also provided a method for public participation in the rulemaking process, standardized the rulemaking process, and confirmed the availability of judicial review of administrative decisions. Federal administrative

13. Significantly, some sources, such as Westlaw, commonly refer to North Carolina "rules" as regulations.

regulations have the full force and effect of law when created within the parameters of the APA.[14]

A. Administrative Regulations

Federal regulations are created in much the same way as North Carolina administrative rules. After receiving authority from enabling statutes passed by Congress to draft rules governing a specific issue, an agency investigates the issue and uses its expertise to propose regulations. The proposed regulations are published in the *Federal Register* to give the public notice. The public then has a specific period of time in which to respond to a proposed regulation. The agency may hold one or more public hearings about the proposed regulations. The public may conveniently find, view, and comment on proposed federal regulations at the Regulations.gov website.[15] Thereafter, the agency considers the public feedback and then issues final regulations, which also must be published in the *Federal Register*. The final regulations are subsequently codified in the *Code of Federal Regulations*.

1. Code of Federal Regulations

The *Code of Federal Regulations* (C.F.R.) is similar to the *North Carolina Administrative Code*. The C.F.R., first published in 1939, is a compilation of all the federal administrative regulations currently in effect. The C.F.R. is published yearly, in quarterly installments, by the Government Publishing Office (GPO). Regulations in the C.F.R. are grouped according to the issuing agency, resulting in a loose arrangement by topic. The C.F.R. contains fifty titles, some of which correspond to the titles of the *United States Code*; for example, in both the *United States Code* and the C.F.R., Title 26 pertains to the Internal Revenue Service. However, even when the titles do not correspond, the *United States Code* is a good source for finding relevant regulations.

Each title of the C.F.R. is organized by chapter, part, and section. For example, in the citation 20 C.F.R. 416.906, 20 is the title, 416 is the part, and .906 is the section. As in the *North Carolina Administrative Code*, chapters in the C.F.R. are often not used in identifying specific regulations. Often, when speaking of the section, the part is included without being stated. A lawyer might say "§ 416.906."

14. *Atchison, T. & S.F. Ry. Co. v. Scarlett*, 300 U.S. 471 (1937).
15. regulations.gov.

The C.F.R. is available in print and online. Though the print volumes are published in quarterly installments,[16] many volumes are published piecemeal at different times—even volumes addressing parts of the same title. Moreover, updates to the volumes are often distributed slowly. Fortunately, the paper covers of the individual volumes change color each year, which makes identifying updated volumes much easier.

The GPO also publishes the C.F.R. on the Govinfo website.[17] Currently, the text of the annual C.F.R. edition at the website is generally no more up to date than the print copy. The GPO also produces the "Electronic Code of Federal Regulations" (e-C.F.R.), which is an authentic but unofficial editorial compilation of the C.F.R. incorporating the latest amendments as published in the *Federal Register*. It is typically updated and current within several days of any changes published in the *Federal Register* affecting currently codified regulations. However, because the e-C.F.R. is not designated as official, it should not be your sole source for researching federal regulations.

Westlaw, Lexis, and Bloomberg also provide fee-based C.F.R. databases that, like GPO's e-C.F.R., are updated within days of changes published in the *Federal Register*. Finally, HeinOnline is an excellent comprehensive source for historical versions of the C.F.R.

2. *Federal Register*

The *Federal Register* serves the same purpose as the *North Carolina Register*. It is published every business day, rather than biweekly like the *North Carolina Register*. All of the issues published within a year make up a single volume. The *Federal Register* serves as the official publication for proposed and final federal regulations, as well as for notices from federal agencies and for some Presidential documents such as executive orders. Its table of contents page provides a list of all of the executive agencies and documents produced by each agency. It also contains helpful finding aids such as an "Index by Subject and

---

16. Titles 1–16 contain regulations in force as of January 1 of the applicable year; Titles 17–27 contain regulations in force as of April 1 of the applicable year; Titles 28–41 contain regulations in force as of July 1 of the applicable year; and Titles 42–50 contain regulations in force as of October 1 of the applicable year.

17. govinfo.gov. Prior to 2010, the GPO website that hosted C.F.R. was GPO Access at www.gpoaccess.gov/C.F.R./index.html. As of December 14, 2018, the Federal Digital System website (gpo.gov/fdsys) was retired.

Name," a "List of C.F.R. Parts Affected" in each daily issue, and a "List of C.F.R. Parts Affected" for the month in the last daily issue of that month.

The *Federal Register* often contains an agency's reasoning behind the regulatory scheme or changes in a section called "Notice of Proposed Rulemaking." In the final version of the regulations, explanations of changes and responses to comments made by the public or interested organizations and businesses are often included. This makes the *Federal Register* a rich source for interpreting the meaning of the regulations and predicting the choices and arguments an agency is likely to make when enforcing the regulations.

The best access to the *Federal Register* is provided online by the publisher, the GPO, on the Govinfo website, where it is updated every day by 6:00 a.m.[18] It is free and is both browsable and searchable. Westlaw, Lexis, and Bloomberg also provide online access through currently updated databases that are fee-based. Again, HeinOnline is an excellent comprehensive source for historical versions of the *Federal Register*.

B. Researching Federal Administrative Regulations

1. Starting with Secondary Sources

For many reasons, print research involving federal regulations can be difficult and very inefficient. As with North Carolina rules, researching federal regulations is best begun in secondary sources. Reading about a legal issue in secondary sources might actually lead you to citations to relevant regulations. And the understanding and terminology you gain from the secondary sources will only improve your ability to conduct effective full-text keyword searches in the C.F.R., if necessary.

2. Using the *United States Code*

Because the *United States Code* is generally easier to search than the C.F.R., the next best starting point to search for relevant regulations would be the *United States Code Service* or the *United States Code Annotated*. These annotated codes provide citations to relevant regulations. Historically, the *United States Code Service* has done a superior job of including references to regulations in the annotations to the statutes.

18. govinfo.gov.

3. Browsing Titles or Searching the Index

Additional options for searching for relevant regulations include browsing the C.F.R. titles and chapters and using the single-volume index at the end of the C.F.R. set. Each option presents challenges. The title names are not always helpful in identifying the scope of regulations they contain. The index only indexes regulations down to the "part" level rather than the "section" level and is notoriously not very detailed. When using the index, you must locate the part and then browse the list of sections in the specific volume to find the most relevant sections.

4. Online Search Options

Because of their frequent (weekly and sometimes even daily) updates, online research methods are more efficient when searching for federal regulations. These online options are plentiful, and they tend to be both more convenient and more productive. The online version of the C.F.R. from the GPO is browsable and searchable by keyword, citation, or title. Because it is directly posted by the GPO and is freely available on the Govinfo website,[19] use of this database is highly recommended. The GPO's Electronic Code of Federal Regulations (e-C.F.R.), available at eCFR.gov, is also useful, especially due to its current updating.

Westlaw, Lexis, and Bloomberg maintain C.F.R. databases that are also currently updated and provide keyword- and title-browsable access. Westlaw provides a browsable index hyperlinked to relevant portions of the C.F.R. This is also an excellent online option for researching regulations.

5. Updating Federal Administrative Regulations

a. Online

Because of the many options and ease of use, online updating is the preferred method of updating federal regulations. The best way to update a federal regulation is to use eCFR.gov as the starting point.[20] This resource provides the date through which the most recent changes to regulations were incorporated into the text. Next, locate the *Federal Register* issues online that have been published since the most recent incorporation date from e-C.F.R.[21] Examine the "C.F.R. Sections Affected" chart in the most recent issue of the

19. govinfo.gov.
20. eCFR.gov.
21. govinfo.gov.

Federal Register to make sure your section has not been amended. A similar method should be used if you choose to update the C.F.R. database on Westlaw, Lexis, or Bloomberg. Very little updating is necessary with the e-C.F.R., Westlaw, Lexis, or Bloomberg databases, as these platforms regularly update their content.

To update the official annual edition of the C.F.R. on GPO's Govinfo website,[22] you must use the "List of Sections Affected" database, which covers the period from the annual edition publication date to the current date. This process is very similar to the process for updating the print version of the C.F.R. Just as with print, any gap in time between the coverage of the "List of Sections Affected" database and the current date must be covered using the daily *Federal Registers*. This process might be more intuitive after reviewing the following explanation of updating the C.F.R. in print.

b. Print

Updating the print version of C.F.R. and the official annual C.F.R. database onlinc[23] arc both cumbersome. Regardless of the source of the annual edition (print or the Govinfo website), and assuming the title you are updating is more than one month past publication, there is a two-step process for updating a paper regulation. The updating process is similar to checking pocket parts, except that you will use a separate publication called the *List of Sections Affected* (LSA) and the back page of the *Federal Register*.

First, find the most recent pamphlet (or database on the Govinfo website) called *List of Sections Affected* (LSA). LSA is a monthly publication that lists all C.F.R. sections affected by recent agency rulemaking activity.[24] Information in LSA should be current back to the publication date of your paper C.F.R. volume; however, you should confirm the dates of coverage for the LSA publication or database to ensure coverage. If there is no reference to a section containing your regulation in LSA, there have been no changes to your regulation between the date the C.F.R. title was last published and the date of the LSA. If, however, there has been a change, LSA will list the *Federal Register* page number for each new agency action that has affected your specific section.

Next, examine the tables called "C.F.R. Parts Affected for [the current month]" located in the back of the *Federal Registers* to find any references to your C.F.R. section. Search the table in each *Federal Register* volume published

22. *Id.*
23. *Id.*
24. The LSA is also available online through govinfo.gov/app/collection/LSA.

on the last day of each month since the most recently published monthly LSA. When you reach the current month, search this same table in the most recent *Federal Register* issue. The chart in the back of the *Federal Register* is always cumulative for the entire month. The paper *Federal Register* will probably be a week or two old due to mailing and processing. However, if you use the free online issues of the *Federal Register* on the Govinfo website, which are updated each morning by 6:00 a.m., this process will update your regulation to same-day currency.[25]

c. Using Citators

In addition to updating the regulations themselves, a researcher should also use citators such as KeyCite on Westlaw or Shepard's on Lexis Advance to find all related information citing a specific regulation being researched.

C. Administrative Decisions

As with North Carolina agencies, federal agencies hold quasi-judicial hearings and issue a number of types and levels of administrative decisions. Federal administrative decisions are, however, much more varied and widely dispersed. Some agencies' decisions are published in print reporters specific to those agencies, while others are not. For example, historically, *Federal Trade Commission Decisions* has been the reporter for the decisions of the Federal Trade Commission. Additionally, until recently, a number of agency decisions were also published in private publications by publishers such as Commerce Clearing House (CCH) and Bureau of National Affairs (BNA). For more information about official and unofficial reporters of agency decisions, and to see a selected list of agency reporters, see Table 1.2 of the *Bluebook*, "Federal Administrative and Executive Materials," and Appendix 7(A) of the *ALWD Guide to Legal Citation*, "Selected Official Federal Administrative and Executive Reporters and Publications."[26]

More recent federal agency decisions are now published directly on the agency's websites. For example, the Federal Trade Commission's website now provides access to its decisions dating back to 1969. Agency websites are independent and also vary widely in terms of how they are organized and what information they provide. You can easily find these websites online using a search engine such as Google. Alternatively, you can consult the collection of links to

25. govinfo.gov.

26. See the *Bluebook*, table T1.2, at 218. See also ALWD & Colleen M. Barger, ALWD Guide to Legal Citation App. 7(A) (6th ed. 2017).

"Administrative Decisions and Other Actions" posted by the University of Virginia Library.[27] This site might be particularly useful if you do not initially know which agency publishes the decisions that are relevant to your research question, or if the agency in question publishes more than one type of decision and you do not know which type is relevant to your research. Recent agency decisions are also selectively available in fee-based databases on Westlaw, Lexis, and Bloomberg.

Once all administrative remedies have been exhausted, unsatisfied parties may have the opportunity to appeal an administrative decision to federal court. Once the issues from a specific administrative decision have been raised in federal court, your research into those issues must include researching case law, which is addressed in Chapters 7 and 8.

IV. Tools for the Toolbox

1. In North Carolina, a "rule" is "any agency regulation, standard, or statement of general applicability that implements or interprets an enactment of the General Assembly or Congress."
2. Researching North Carolina and federal regulations is best begun in secondary sources, where you may find citations to relevant regulations.
3. Annotated codes provide an excellent starting point for finding a particular rule when the authority for the rule is already known.
4. Because of the many options and ease of use, online updating is the preferred method to update federal regulations. The best way to update a federal regulation is to use e-C.F.R., located at eCFR.gov, as the starting point.

27. guides.lib.virginia.edu/administrative_decisions.

Chapter Seven

Court Systems and Reporters

Many, if not most, research questions require you to consult judicial opinions (case law) to determine what the governing legal rules are and how those rules apply to the questions at hand. When there is no statute that governs your research question, case law will likely be the sole source of relevant primary authority. Even when you find a statute (and perhaps administrative materials) addressing your research question, you must often consult caselaw to understand what they mean and how they apply to your research question.

Building on the introductory materials in Chapter 1, this chapter provides an in-depth discussion of the North Carolina and federal court systems and describes the various reporters and databases that contain the opinions of the courts in those systems. This chapter also describes the most important features of published cases, some of which are added by publishers as editorial enhancements, and offers strategies for finding, reading, and understanding cases.

I. Court Systems

Historically speaking, our American judicial system is based on the English common law judicial system. Significantly, long after gaining independence, America has held to the common law system, and it has continued to develop.

As noted in Chapter 1, the basic court structure in most states and in the federal system includes a trial court, an intermediate appellate court, and an ultimate appellate court, often called the *supreme court*. Notably, due to the concept of *stare decisis*[1] in the common law system, decisions of appellate courts must be followed by lower courts in the same jurisdiction. Trial court

1. *Stare decisis* is a Latin phrase meaning to "to stand by things decided." In the legal context, *stare decisis* represents the doctrine of precedent, requiring courts to follow earlier judicial decisions of higher courts in the same jurisdiction when the same points of law are addressed. *Stare decisis*, *Black's Law Dictionary* 1626 (10th ed. 2014).

decisions, therefore, have little or no precedential value, and they are typically not published.[2]

A. Federal Courts Relevant to North Carolina Practitioners and Researchers

1. United States District Courts

The federal trial court is called the United States District Court, which has original jurisdiction in most federal cases, civil and criminal. The trials may be by jury or bench (judge only). North Carolina has three District Courts: the United States District Court for the Western District of North Carolina (based in Charlotte); the United States District Court for the Middle District of North Carolina (based in Greensboro); and the United States District Court for the Eastern District of North Carolina (based in Raleigh).

2. United States Courts of Appeals

The ninety-four federal districts are organized into twelve regional circuits. Each circuit includes a Court of Appeals serving as the intermediate appellate court for all District Courts within that circuit. A thirteenth Court of Appeals, the Court of Appeals for the Federal Circuit, has appellate jurisdiction over limited specialized subjects such as patents and certain money claims against the United States government.

North Carolina is in the Fourth Circuit, and appeals from the United States District Courts in North Carolina are appealed to the United States Court of Appeals for the Fourth Circuit, based in Richmond, Virginia. See Appendix C, Geographic Boundaries of the United States Judicial System, for a map of the federal judicial system's geographical boundaries.

---

2. State trial courts issue orders and judgments containing the courts' findings of fact and conclusions of law in the specific cases they hear. These orders and judgments are not referred to as *opinions*; moreover, they are binding only on the parties to each case, and they are not published. Federal district (trial) courts do issue opinions, some of which are published in the *Federal Supplement* or *Federal Appendix* reporters; many other federal district court opinions are unpublished.

3. Supreme Court of the United States

The highest federal court is the Supreme Court of the United States. While the Court receives approximately 7,500 petitions for writ of certiorari (requests for appeals to be heard) per year, fewer than 200 cases are accepted for review, and of those, only about eighty cases receive full (plenary) review with oral arguments from attorneys. The accepted cases may have originated in the federal courts or may have been appealed from state supreme courts. The accepted cases usually involve important issues arising under the U.S. Constitution or other federal law, or issues that have been decided differently by the Circuit Courts of Appeals (referred to as a "circuit split").

B. North Carolina State Courts

The North Carolina state court system is similar to the three-tiered federal court system; it has several trial courts, an intermediate court of appeals, and a supreme court.

1. Trial Courts in North Carolina

The District Court is the lower of the two trial courts in North Carolina. Its jurisdiction includes civil cases involving less than $10,000, family law cases, criminal cases involving misdemeanors and infractions, and juvenile cases. Small claims court is a subdivision of the District Court and hears matters involving less than $5,000 where parties are typically not represented by an attorney. Jury trials are not offered in District Court. At least one District Court sits in each of North Carolina's 100 counties, usually in the county seat.

The Superior Court is the higher of the two trial courts in North Carolina. The state's 100 counties are divided into forty-six Superior Court districts. Superior Court jurisdiction includes civil cases involving more than $10,000, all felony criminal cases, misdemeanor criminal cases appealed from a District Court, and appeals from North Carolina administrative agency decisions. A twelve-member jury hears cases in Superior Court, although jury trials may be waived. In jury trials, generally, the jury determines questions of fact and the presiding judge determines questions of law. In trials without a jury, the judge determines both the facts and the law.

2. North Carolina Court of Appeals

The North Carolina Court of Appeals became operational in October 1967, after voters overwhelmingly approved a proposed amendment to Article IV of the North Carolina Constitution. The amendment authorized an intermediate appellate court to relieve the caseload pressure on the Supreme Court, which until that time handled all appeals from trial courts. Initially composed of nine judges,[3] the Court of Appeals is currently composed of 15 judges who typically sit in rotating panels of three. However, in 2017, the General Assembly voted to reduce the Court of Appeals to twelve.[4]

3. North Carolina Supreme Court

Six Associate Justices and the Chief Justice comprise the North Carolina Supreme Court. Like the Court of Appeals, the Supreme Court reviews only questions of law rather than facts, which have already been determined at the trial level.

In several types of cases, and as provided by statute, an appellant has a statutory right of appeal to the Supreme Court: cases involving constitutional questions; cases from the Court of Appeals that include dissenting opinions; or cases concerning the bar exam, judicial standards, or a utilities commission rate.[5] The Supreme Court may also accept an appeal within its discretion in cases involving a significant public interest and cases construing major legal principles.[6] Figure 7-1 illustrates the routes of appeal in North Carolina state courts.

II. Publication of Judicial Opinions

As briefly discussed in Chapter 1, a judicial opinion, usually called a case, is written by a court to explain its decision in a particular legal dispute.[7] While

---

3. N.C. Gen. Stat. § 7A-16 (2017). Note that the law creating the Court in 1967 provided for six judges, but allowed for its immediate expansion on July 1, 1969 by the Governor's appointment of three additional judges. David Britt updated by Robert N. Hunter, Jr., History of the Court of Appeals of North Carolina July 1967—March 2016 (2016), celebrate.nccourts.org/sites/default/files/HISTORY_OF_COA_3_Mar_2016.pdf.

4. N.C. Gen. Stat. § 7A-16 (2017) (As judges retire, they will not be replaced until the number of seated judges reaches the statutorily mandated 12 judges.).

5. N.C. Gen. Stat. §§ 7A-27, -29, -30 (2017).

6. N.C. Gen. Stat. § 7A-31 (2017).

7. Cases may be civil, criminal, or administrative in nature. Civil cases are initiated by one or more private citizens (plaintiffs) against other citizens or entities (defendants) seeking some type of remedy or redress for a perceived wrong. Remedies in civil cases may include monetary damages, declaratory relief (i.e., a determination of the rights of the parties involved), or injunctive relief (i.e., ordering the defendant to stop doing something). Criminal cases are brought by the state or federal government for violation

millions of cases (criminal and civil) are initiated across the United States every year, with a significant number being appealed by the losing party, only those cases in which appellate courts render a written opinion are typically published.[8] The courts' opinions in those cases are published in books called *reporters*.[9] Reporters publish opinions in chronological order by the date of issuance.

A reporter may include cases from several courts within a particular geographical region, cases from a single court, or both. For example, the *South Eastern Reporter Series* publishes state court decisions from North Carolina, Georgia, South Carolina, Virginia, and West Virginia. The *North Carolina Supreme Court Reporter* publishes only the decisions of the North Carolina Supreme Court, and the *United States Reports* publishes only the decisions of the Supreme Court of the United States. Other reporters publish only cases in a certain subject area, such as bankruptcy or tax.

Initially, the responsibility for reporting decisions of the courts rested with individuals rather than corporations. In those early days, a particular person, who was appointed by the court, was responsible for recording and publishing that court's decisions. The books that those persons generated were generically referred to as "nominative reporters."

Eventually, courts began to enter into agreements with publishers who could provide more services than just reporting what the judges wrote. These publishers began providing editorial enhancements, such as identifying important

---

of a penal law by an alleged offender (defendant). The remedies available in criminal cases include fines payable to the government and/or imprisonment. Administrative cases are addressed separately in Chapter 8.

8. Here, the term "published" means designated for publication in an official reporter. In section E of this chapter, the term "published" is discussed as a function of an opinion's precedential value. Today there is really no such thing as an "unpublished" opinion, because even cases that are designated "not for publication" by the issuing courts are published on commercial platforms like Westlaw and Lexis. "Unpublished" opinions are not binding, and courts within the particular jurisdiction need not follow them in subsequent decisions. Indeed, in the past, procedural rules in most jurisdictions forbade, or at least disfavored, citation to such opinions.

9. Reporters are widely accessible to law students and lawyers, both in print and online, and collectively, their contents make up the body of law known as "case law." A reporter that has been designated by the courts of a jurisdiction to publish their opinions is called an *official reporter*. Other reporters that have not been so designated are called *unofficial reporters*. For example, North Carolina has designated Lexis's *North Carolina Reports* (abbreviated "N.C.") as the official reporter for North Carolina Supreme Court opinions; *West's Southeastern Reporter* series is the unofficial reporter for those opinions.

Figure 7-1. North Carolina Courts System Routes of Appeal

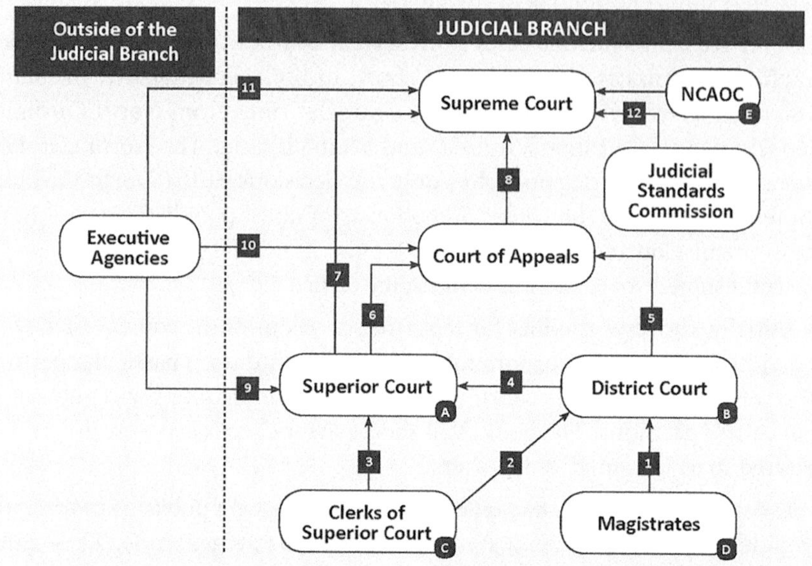

A. Superior courts have original jurisdiction over all felony cases and civil cases in which the amount in controversy exceeds $25,000.*

B. District courts have original jurisdiction over misdemeanor cases not assigned to magistrates; probable cause hearings; accept guilty / no contest pleas in certain felony cases; civil cases in which the amount in controversy is $25,000 or less;* juvenile proceedings; domestic relations; mental health hospital commitments.

C. Clerks of superior court have original jurisdiction over probate and estates, certain special proceedings (condemnations, adoptions, partitions, foreclosures, etc.); in certain cases, may accept guilty pleas or admissions of responsibility and enter judgment.

D. Magistrates have original jurisdiction to accept certain misdemeanor guilty pleas and admission of responsibility to infractions; worthless check misdemeanors valued at $2,000 or less; small claims in which the amount in controversy is $10,000 or less; valuation of property in certain estate cases.

E. The Chief Justice appoints the Director of the North Carolina Administrative Office of the Courts (NCAOC). The NCAOC serves the Judicial Branch through Budget Management; Communications; Court Programs and Services; Financial Services; General Counsel; General Services; Governmental Affairs; Human Resources; Judicial Fellowship; Research, Policy, and Planning; Technology Services; and Training and Development.

1. Most appeals from magistrates go to the district court for de novo proceedings.
2. Appeals involving adoptions; appeals of foreclosures of a certain jurisdictional amount may go to the district court.
3. All appeals not handled by the district court.
4. Appeals in all criminal cases for de novo trial.
5. Appeals in all civil and juvenile cases.
6. All appeals that do not proceed directly to the Supreme Court.
7. Appeals in cases in which a first-degree murder defendant has been sentenced to death. Appeals from the Business Court. Appeals in redistricting cases. The Supreme Court conducts discretionary review of appeals directly from the trial courts in cases of significant public interest, in cases involving legal principles of major significance, in cases where delay would cause substantial harm, or in cases where the Court of Appeals docket is unusually full.
8. Appeal of right exists in cases involving certain constitutional questions and in cases in which there has been a dissent in the Court of Appeals. The Supreme Court also conducts discretionary review of appeals from the Court of Appeals in cases of significant public interest, in cases involving legal principles of major significance, in cases where delay would cause substantial harm, or in cases where the Court of Appeals docket is unusually full.
9. Appeals from administrative decisions that do not proceed directly to the Supreme Court or the Court of Appeals.
10. Appeals of the Industrial Commission, the North Carolina State Bar, the Property Tax Commission, the Commissioner of Insurance, the Department of Health and Human Services, the Secretary of Environmental Quality, and the Utilities Commission (in decisions other than general rate cases).
11. Appeals of final orders of the Utilities Commission in general rate cases.
12. Recommendations from the Commission for removal, suspension, censure, or public reprimand.

*The district and superior courts have concurrent original jurisdiction in civil actions (G.S. 7A-240). The small claims court is the proper division for the trial of civil actions in which the amount in controversy is $10,000 or less, and the district court division is the proper division for matters of $25,000 or less (G.S. 7A-243); the superior court division is the proper division for matters exceeding $25,000 in controversy.

Source: Used with permission of the North Carolina Administrative Office of the Courts.

points of law from each case for indexing purposes. Synopses of the cases were often added at the beginning of the cases to help researchers quickly understand what issues the cases addressed.

This pattern of publication continues today, with corporations having taken over the publishing duties. Over 100 years ago, the West Publishing Company began a large-scale project of publishing every state's appellate court opinions and providing significant editorial enhancements in regional reporters. Some states publish their own print reporters or contract with other publishers to do so. Every case citation includes at least one reporter volume, reporter name, and page number. Thus, every researcher must be familiar with the reporter system to find relevant cases, whether in print or online. Chapter 10 discusses proper citation format for cases.

A. Characteristics of Reporters

1. Advance Sheets

All hardbound volumes of case reporters are periodically updated by *advance sheet pamphlets*. Advance sheets include the cases already prepared with headnotes (discussed below) and the pagination that will exist when the cases are published in the next hardbound volume. Once enough cases have been issued to comprise the next hardbound volume, that volume is published, and the associated advance sheets are removed from the shelf.

2. Tables

The reporters have information, often in tabular form, at the beginning and/or end of each volume. Typically, the tables might include a list of the judges on the bench at the time the opinions in the volume were issued, a list of the cases in the volume arranged in alphabetical order, and some type of subject index. In the *South Eastern Reporter*, the unofficial reporter where North Carolina state court opinions are published, all of the cases in each volume have been digested using the West Topic and Key Number System, which will be explained in Part III of this chapter.

3. Reporter Series

Reporter publishers often choose to end a series of volumes at a particular point. They then begin a second series of the reporter. For example, West ended the first series of the *South Eastern Reporter* in 1939 at volume 200 and began the second series. A researcher must thus know the series of the *South Eastern Reporter* along with the volume and page number.

B. Publication of North Carolina State Court Decisions

Like federal (and other state) appellate courts, North Carolina appellate courts issue written decisions, most of which are published in reporters. Because it takes time for these decisions to be published in hardbound volumes, they are generally available sooner from other sources. First, appellate court decisions can be obtained from the courts themselves, on ordinary 8½ x 11-inch paper; these are known as *slip opinions* or *slip decisions*. In addition, North Carolina appellate courts now publish their opinions at the website of the North Carolina Judicial Branch.[10]

After some time, the printed slip opinions are gathered together and printed in softbound pamphlets called *advance sheets*. Advance sheets are printed every week or so in "advance" of the hardbound volumes of the official and unofficial reporters and are issued to libraries and other reporter subscribers. They contain the full text of approximately twenty to thirty opinions, and they often include the dispositions of many other cases in which the court did not publish an opinion. Significantly, each case looks exactly as it will ultimately appear in the hardbound reporter, including the same text, typeface, and page numbers. Advance sheets for opinions of both the North Carolina Supreme Court and the North Carolina Court of Appeals are typically found in black loose-leaf binders located after the most recently published hardbound reporter on the shelf.

1. Official Reporters

a. North Carolina Reports

The *North Carolina Reports*, published by Lexis, is the official reporter of North Carolina Supreme Court decisions. Lexis editors analyze each case, identify the points of law from the case, summarize each point in a paragraph called a *headnote*, and place those headnotes at the beginning of the case.

---

10. nccourts.gov/documents/opinions. Court of Appeals cases are available on the Administrative Office of the Courts website from 1996 forward, and Supreme Court cases are available from 1997 forward. Anyone with Internet access can retrieve these opinions. No subscription is needed; nor is access to Westlaw, Lexis, or Bloomberg required.

b. North Carolina Court of Appeals Reports

Lexis also publishes the North Carolina Court of Appeals' official reporter, the *North Carolina Court of Appeals Reports.* As with the *North Carolina Reports,* the *North Carolina Court of Appeals Reports* includes unique headnotes identifying the main points of law at the beginning of each case. The *North Carolina Court of Appeals Reports* began publication when that Court originated in 1967.

2. Unofficial Reporters

In addition to the official reporters of North Carolina judicial opinions, there are also unofficial reporters publishing these same cases. In the 1880s, the West Publishing Company (now West, a Thomson Reuters business) began publishing a series of regional reporters. Dividing the nation into regions, each regional reporter set publishes appellate decisions from all the states in that region.

a. West's South Eastern Reporter

West's South Eastern Reporter[11] began publication in 1887 and includes the court of appeals and supreme court decisions from the states of North Carolina, Georgia, South Carolina, Virginia, and West Virginia. The *South Eastern Reporter* began when volume 96 of the *North Carolina Reports* was being published. Cases have been duplicated in both reporters since 1887. The *South Eastern Reporter* is published in an original series (S.E.), which consists of 200 volumes, including cases up to early 1939, and a second series (S.E.2d), which currently consists of more than 600 volumes. Advance sheets for the *South Eastern Reporter (Second Series)* are published approximately once a week.

One major advantage of using the West regional reporters is that the headnotes found at the beginning of each case are connected to the Topic and Key Numbers of the West Digest System. For a discussion about the West Topic and Key Number System, see Section III of Chapter 8.

b. North Carolina Reporter

A *South Eastern Reporter* offprint, the *North Carolina Reporter,* contains only North Carolina court decisions, exactly as they appear in the *South Eastern Reporter.* Because the pagination is identical to *South Eastern Reporter,* pagi-

---

11. The *South Eastern Reporter* is one of seven regional reporters published by West covering state court opinions from each of the fifty states: the Atlantic (A), North Eastern (N.E.), North Western (N.W), Pacific (P.), Southern (So.), South Western (S.W.), and South Eastern (S.E.).

nation gaps exist in the *North Carolina Reporter* where the other states' cases were printed in *South Eastern Reporter*. Significantly, the *North Carolina Reporter* might be more useful than the *South Eastern Reporter* to a researcher who is concerned only with North Carolina case law.

3. Online Publication of North Carolina Cases

a. Fee-Based Sources

The publishers listed in Table 7-1 provide access to North Carolina judicial decisions for a fee. All of these companies provide very quick access to newly issued cases.

Table 7-1. Online Providers of North Carolina Cases

Westlaw
www.westlaw.com

"North Carolina State Cases" on Westlaw contains cases from the North Carolina state courts from 1778 to date. It is typically updated within hours or a few days of the issuance of new opinions.

Lexis
www.advance.lexis.com

North Carolina cases can be found in a database with coverage back to 1778. It is typically updated within hours or a few days of the issuance of new opinions.

Bloomberg
www.bloomberglaw.com

Locate the database from the main page by selecting the "Court Opinions" link and entering "North Carolina" in the "Select Sources" box. This database contains North Carolina cases since 1778. It is typically updated quickly after the issuance of new opinions.

Fastcase
www.fastcase.com

North Carolina appellate cases are covered back to 1778. While Fastcase is not a free legal research service, the North Carolina Bar Association provides free Fastcase access to Bar Association members.

b. Free Sources

i. North Carolina Administrative Office of the Courts Website

The North Carolina Administrative Office of the Courts publishes the slip opinions from the Supreme Court and the Court of Appeals back to 1998 on its North Carolina Court System website.[12] The opinions are posted at least once a month. The opinions are posted in reverse chronological order by year. In addition to a browsing feature, the database includes a basic search function. The cases can be accessed and downloaded for free. However, there are no editorial enhancements such as an editor's synopsis or headnotes at the beginning of the cases.

ii. North Carolina Cases from Other Websites

Other well-known law-related websites such as Cornell Law School's Legal Information Institute[13] and FindLaw[14] provide links to North Carolina cases. However, these legal mega-sites simply link directly to the North Carolina Administrative Office of the Courts website discussed above, rather than providing their own databases of North Carolina cases.

C. Publication of Federal Court Decisions

1. Print Publications

Federal court opinions are available for United States District (trial) Courts, the Unted States Courts of Appeals, and the Supreme Court of the United States. Federal cases are primarily published by West, Lexis, and other private publishers. See Table 7-2 for an overview of the Federal courts and the corresponding reporters that publish their opinions.

a. Reporters for Federal Cases

i. Federal Supplement

United States District Court opinions have been published by West in the *Federal Supplement* since its inception in 1932. Although the federal government has not designated an official government reporter for United States District Court opinions, the *Federal Supplement* is used and cited in most, if not all, courts. Selected District Court opinions from all over the country, including North Carolina's three federal District Courts, are reported chronologically in

12. appellate.nccourts.org/opinions.
13. law.cornell.edu.
14. lp.findlaw.com.

Table 7-2. Summary of Reporters for Federal Court Cases

Court	Reporter Name	Abbreviations
Supreme Court	United States Reports (official) Supreme Court Reporter United States Supreme Court Reports, Lawyers' Edition	U.S. S. Ct. L. Ed., L. Ed. 2d
Courts of Appeals	Federal Reporter, 1880– Federal Cases, 1789–1879 Federal Appendix, 2001–	F., F.2d, F.3d F. Cas. F. App'x
District Courts	Federal Supplement, 1932– Federal Rules Decisions, 1940– (limited coverage)	F. Supp., F. Supp. 2d, F. Supp. 3d F.R.D.

the *Federal Supplement.* The following list shows the dates of coverage by series:

Federal Supplement, 3d	2014–
Federal Supplement, 2d	1998–2014
Federal Supplement	1932–1998

ii. Federal Rules Decisions

The *Federal Rules Decisions* is published by West and contains only United States District Court decisions construing the Federal Rules of Civil Procedure, the Federal Rules of Criminal Procedure, the Federal Rules of Appellate Procedure, and the Federal Rules of Evidence that are not reported in the *Federal Supplement.*

iii. Federal Reporter

The majority of United States Court of Appeals decisions are designated for publication in the *Federal Reporter.* (Those that have not been so designated have been published in the *Federal Appendix* since 2001.) The *Federal Reporter,* which has been in publication since 1880, is published by West. Researchers interested in United States Court of Appeals decisions affecting North Carolina can find opinions from the Fourth Circuit Court of Appeals in this reporter. The following list shows the dates of coverage by series:

Federal Reporter, 3d	1993–
Federal Reporter, 2d	1925–1993
Federal Reporter	1880–1925

iv. Federal Appendix

This unofficial West reporter, published since 2001, includes cases from the United States Courts of Appeals that were not designated for publication in the *Federal Reporter* and are therefore "unpublished." Section E below explains the distinction between "published" and "unpublished" cases.

v. Federal Cases

Federal Cases is a collection of thirty volumes and a digest that reports United States Circuit Court decisions "from the earliest times to the beginning of the federal reporter." Coverage dates are 1789 to 1879. The set was published between 1894 and 1897 by West.

vi. *United States Reports*

The *United States Reports* is the official reporter of opinions of the Supreme Court of the United States and is published by the Government Publishing Office. Practically speaking, this reporter is rarely used for research purposes because it is a such a slow publication, lagging at least three or four years behind in its publication cycle and because it offers no editorial enhancements. However, since it is the official reporter of Supreme Court decisions, most citation rules require citation to the *United States Reports*, if the case appears in it.

Early in the Court's history, there was no official reporter of its decisions. Instead, the first volumes were privately reported (nominative reporters) and still bear the names of the reporters, such as Dallas, Cranch, and Wheaton, even though they have now been incorporated into the *United States Reports*.

vii. *United States Supreme Court Reports, Lawyers' Edition*

The *United States Supreme Court Reports, Lawyer's Edition* is a privately published reporter that provides complete coverage of opinions of the Supreme Court of the United States. Now published by Lexis, the reporter has traditionally offered editorial enhancements such as summaries of briefs submitted to the Court and articles written by editorial staff addressing the legal topics from the decision for selected cases.

viii. West's Supreme Court Reporter

The *Supreme Court Reporter* is published by West and began covering Supreme Court decisions in 1882. The cases include traditional West enhancements such as headnotes connected to the West Topic and Key Number System.

b. Advance Sheets

Each print report is accompanied by advance sheets containing new opinions, usually within four to six weeks of their filing. These pamphlets include the cases already prepared with headnotes and the pagination that will exist when the cases are published in the next hardbound volume. Those Court of Appeals decisions not selected for publication might be selected for the *Federal Appendix* and would appear in advance sheets for that reporter. Eventually, cases published in advance sheets are incorporated into a new volume of the reporter, and the advance sheets are discarded.

2. Online Publication

The same publishers listed in Table 7-1 as providing access to North Carolina cases also provide access to federal cases for a fee. They all provide comprehensive coverage of cases heard in federal courts in North Carolina.

The websites of all three United States District Courts in North Carolina link to recent decisions from the courts.[15] These decisions are in the nature of slip opinions. They are free but lack any editorial enhancements and usually represent a selected collection of recent decisions. If the decisions are not posted on the court's website, the website might link the user to PACER, the federal "Public Access to Court Electronic Records" website where court documents can be downloaded for a minimal charge.[16] The United States Court of Appeals for the Fourth Circuit also frequently posts its decisions in PDF format at the court's website.[17] The Supreme Court of the United States frequently posts its decisions in PDF format at the Court's website.[18]

---

15. Western District at ncwd.uscourts.gov; Middle District at ncmd.uscourts.gov; and Eastern District at nced.uscourts.gov.

16. pacer.gov.

17. ca4.uscourts.gov.

18. supremecourtus.gov.

D. Published vs. Unpublished

Appellate courts have discretion to determine the precedential value of the cases they decide. When a court decides that a case lacks precedential value and does not merit publication in a reporter, that case is designated as an "unpublished" (or "unreported") case.[19] Unpublished decisions have been distributed for years and are widely available online. However, the treatment of unpublished cases often varies because the rules of appellate procedure, which govern their treatment, differ among jurisdictions.

In North Carolina, Rule 30(e) of the North Carolina Rules of Appellate Procedure states, "An unpublished decision of the North Carolina Court of Appeals does not constitute controlling legal authority."[20] Rule 30(e) also notes that the citation to unpublished opinions in North Carolina trial or appellate courts is "disfavored."[21] However, "[i]f a party believes, nevertheless, that an unpublished opinion has precedential value to a material issue in the case and that there is no published opinion that would serve as well, the party may cite the unpublished opinion[.]"[22] The citing party must disclose that the opinion is unpublished and must serve a copy on all parties. Ultimately, a judge decides the case's precedential value to the case being litigated.[23]

Like state cases, federal cases may be designated as either published or unpublished, depending upon a judge's preference or the potential precedential value. A small number of federal District Court decisions are published. A slightly higher number of federal Court of Appeals decisions are published.[24] All opinions of the Supreme Court of the United States are published.

---

19. Today there is really no such thing as an "unpublished" opinion, because even cases that are designated "not for publication" by the issuing courts are published on commercial platforms like Westlaw and Lexis. Unpublished opinions are not binding, as courts within the particular jurisdiction need not follow them in subsequent decisions. Indeed, in the past, procedural rules in most jurisdictions forbade, or at least disfavored, citation to such opinions. Significantly, courts still use the term "published" to describe those cases that are printed in full in an official or unofficial reporter of a particular jurisdiction and that carry precedential value.

20. N.C. R. App. P. 30(e).

21. *Id.*

22. *Id.*

23. *Id.*

24. The U.S. Courts website, https://www.uscourts.gov/sites/default/files/data_tables/jff_2.5_0930.2018.pdf, indicates that in 2018, only 12% of all U.S. Court of Appeals decisions were published.

Prior to 2007, the rules in the various federal circuits treated the use of unreported decisions differently. Some circuits prohibited citation to unpublished opinions, while some circuits allowed it. The question was settled in December 2006 when the Federal Rules of Appellate Procedure were amended to add Rule 32.1. That rule provides that a federal court may not prohibit or restrict the citation of federal judicial opinions that have been designated as unpublished and issued on or after January 1, 2007.[25] If the decision is not available in a publicly accessible electronic database, the citing party must file a copy with the court and serve a copy on all other the parties.[26] As with the North Carolina rule, the federal rule does not address what weight the court must give the unpublished decision.

E. Parts of a Reported Case

Published cases have certain features in common, whether they appear in an official reporter, in a regional reporter, on Westlaw, Lexis, or Bloomberg, on one of the lower cost fee-based services, or on a court's free website. The actual text of the decision should be identical, regardless of where the user accesses it. Beyond that, however, there may be stylistic and formatting differences as well as different levels of enhancements.

Most reports contain the following features for each case:

> ***Parallel Citations.***[27] The cases in most jurisdictions are published in more than one print reporter. For example, North Carolina Supreme Court decisions are reported in the official *North Carolina Reports* and the unofficial *South Eastern Reporter*. While the text of the decision is identical in both reporters, the editorial enhancements are different. Cases reported in the *South Eastern Reporter* include the parallel citation to the official reporter as well.

---

25. Fed. R. App. P. 32.1.

26. *Id.*

27. Chapter 10 includes general information about citation and specific information about parallel citation.

Parties and Procedural Designations. The parties involved in the litigation are listed at the beginning of the case. Procedural designations such as *appellant* and *appellee* may also be included by some editors.

Docket Number. Each court assigns a unique docket number to a case when it is filed with the court. The number functions much like a name, providing a way to organize, identify, and locate all documents related to the case.

Court and Date. The court issuing the opinion and the date of the opinion are listed.

Synopsis. One of the significant editorial enhancements provided by most publishers is a *synopsis* of the case. The synopsis usually summarizes the facts, the procedural posture of the case, the important legal issues involved, and the disposition. A synopsis thus provides a quick overview of the case that allows a researcher to determine the relevance of the case to the legal question she is researching and to assess whether she should spend time reading the case. Sometimes the court's decision will include a synopsis by the judge or justice writing the opinion; this synopsis will be available in the version of the opinion posted on a free court website. Cases available on other freely accessible media do not have synopses.

Disposition. A court's ultimate decision, the *disposition*, is often stated immediately after the synopsis in a reported case. The court may decide to affirm the lower court's ruling. However, if the appellate court disagrees, it may decide to reverse, remand, or vacate the decision. Occasionally, a court may agree with only part of a lower court's decision. In that instance, the court will affirm in part and reverse in part.

Headnotes. Every case involves at least one legal issue and often involves several. When accessing a case from a print reporter, Westlaw, or Lexis, you will note that editors provide a short paragraph setting out each point of law from the case and arrange the paragraphs at the beginning of the case. These paragraphs are called *headnotes*. Containing more detail than the synopsis, these headnotes provide a quick window into the various legal issues involved in the case. Some publishers use the exact language from the text of the case in the headnotes. Other publishers standardize the language in the headnotes, using words that are more generic and likely to also appear in other similar cases. Each headnote begins with a number. Locating that number in the text of the opinion identifies the part of the opinion discussing that point of law. In online services such as Westlaw and Lexis, these numbers are hyperlinked to the relevant part of the case where that point of law is discussed.

Headnote captions may be linked to a case-finding index or digest. The best known of these is West's Topic and Key Number Digest System, which is available in print as well as on Westlaw. See Chapter 8 for more information on this system. The headnotes of North Carolina cases reported in the *South Eastern Reporter* are part of the West Topic and Key Number Digest System.

Opinion. Following all of the editorial enhancements is the text of the court's opinion. Before you can determine whether a case is useful for your research problem, you must read the actual text of the opinion. If the decision is not unanimous, a case may have more than one opinion: a *majority opinion*, with which the majority of judges agree; and either a *concurring opinion*, in which one or more judges agree with the decision of the majority but not the reasoning; a *dissenting opinion*, in which a judge disagrees with the majority's decision; or both. The majority opinion becomes binding precedent. At some future time, a well-crafted dissenting opinion may become useful as an artful statement of the opposing view for litigants hoping to reverse the majority opinion. If there is no majority agreement on the reasoning of a decision, but a majority of judges reaches the same decision, the court's decision is a *plurality opinion*.

To examine and understand some of the various enhancements, see Figure 7-2, a case excerpt from the *South Eastern Reporter*, and Figure 7-3, an excerpt from the same case displayed in Westlaw.

Figure 7-2. Example of a North Carolina Supreme Court Case Viewed in West's *South Eastern*

420 N.C. **352 SOUTH EASTERN REPORTER, 2d SERIES**

brought by the State pursuant to requirements of the AFDC program to collect a debt owed to the State for past public assistance and to obtain a judgment for future child support. The decision of the Court of Appeals is therefore affirmed in part and reversed in part.

This cause is remanded to the Court of Appeals for further remand to the trial court for further proceedings not inconsistent with this opinion. Upon remand, if paternity is contested, the plaintiff may apply to the Superior Court, Jackson County, for a stay of proceedings in that court pending the filing and final disposition of an appropriate proceeding in the Court of Indian Offenses to determine the paternity of the child.

AFFIRMED IN PART, REVERSED IN PART AND REMANDED.

WEBB and WHICHARD, JJ., did not participate in the consideration or decision of this case.

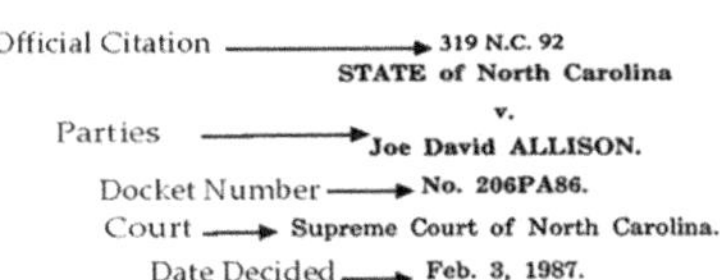

Official Citation → 319 N.C. 92

STATE of North Carolina

v.

Parties → **Joe David ALLISON.**

Docket Number → **No. 206PA86.**

Court → **Supreme Court of North Carolina.**

Date Decided → **Feb. 3, 1987.**

Synopsis → Defendant was convicted in the Superior Court, Gaston County, of attempted robbery with a dangerous weapon. Defendant appealed. The Court of Appeals, 73 N.C. App. 334, 327 S.E.2d 69, found no error. Petition for certiorari was granted. The Supreme Court, Frye, J., held that evidence did not sustain conviction.

Disposition → **Reversed.**

Headnote →

1. Criminal Law ⟹**44**

One element of attempt to commit crime is that defendant have intent to commit substantive offense.

2. Robbery ⟹**12**

Attempted robbery with dangerous weapon occurs when person, with specific intent to unlawfully deprive another of personal property by endangering or threatening his life with dangerous weapon, does some overt act calculated to bring about that result.

3. Robbery ⟹**24.2**

Uncontradicted evidence that defendant informed police of intended robbery beforehand and later assisted police in gathering evidence did not permit reasonable inference that defendant had specific intent to unlawfully deprive store owner of his property and did not support conviction for attempted robbery with a dangerous weapon.

4. Criminal Law ⟹**556**

State ordinarily is not bound by adverse testimony of its witnesses but may offer other contradicting evidence.

On grant of a writ of certiorari to review an unpublished decision of the Court of Appeals, filed 5 March 1985, 73 N.C.App. 334, 327 S.E.2d 69 which found no error in ← Procedural Designation defendant's trial before Beaty, J., and a jury, at the 28 November 1983 Criminal Session of Superior Court, Gaston County. Heard in the Supreme Court 10 December 1986.

Lacy H. Thornburg, Atty. Gen. by T. Buie Costen, Sp. Deputy Atty. Gen., Raleigh, for State. ← Attorneys

Richard A. Rosen, Director, Clinical Program, UNC School of Law, Chapel Hill and Dorothy V. Kibler, Raleigh, for defendant-appellant.

FRYE, Justice. ← Judge

Defendant raised two questions before this Court: (1) whether the trial court erred ← Opinion

Source: West Southeastern Reporter. Reprinted with permission of Thomson-Reuters.

Figure 7-3. Example of the Same North Carolina Supreme Court Case View in Westlaw

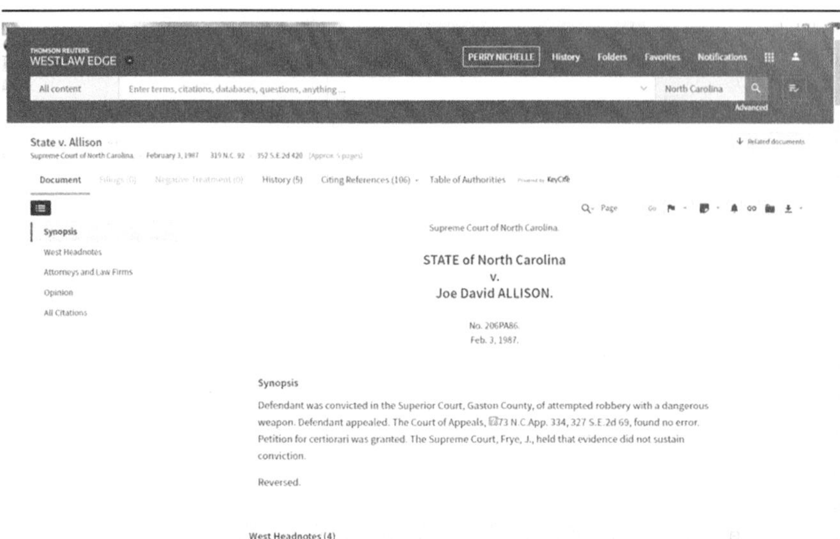

Source Westlaw. Reprinted with permission of Thomson Reuters.

III. Tools for the Toolbox

1. Court opinions, also called cases, are typically published in reporters, which are now available via online databases.
2. Court opinions are also available for free online at state and federal court websites.
3. Whether found in print or online, court opinions contain many of the same parts.

Chapter Eight

Finding and Updating Cases

This chapter addresses how to find cases in print and online, with a particular focus on finding cases by topic. This chapter also discusses updating your case law research. Updating your research is an essential research task; a lawyer must know whether the authority she is relying on is still "good law."

I. Finding Cases

There are many methods of finding cases. Chapter 2 dealt with generating search terms for your research. Chapter 3 discussed how researching a topic in secondary sources such as an encyclopedia, a treatise discussing a specific subject (especially one focused on the relevant jurisdiction), or an *American Law Reports* annotation can lead you to relevant cases. The easiest way to find a case, however, is to use a known citation. Unfortunately, you will rarely begin your work with citations to cases that are directly applicable to your research situations. Thus, you must often locate a case by topic or subject.

The remainder of this chapter addresses finding cases by subject using the West Digest System as well as other case finding tools available on Westlaw, Lexis, and Bloomberg.

A. The Digest System

Case reporters organize cases in chronological order, not by subject. Thus, if you are interested in searching for cases by subject, you must use the research tool that organizes cases by subject, known as a *digest*. A digest is a topical case index for case reporters. The best known and most widely available case law digest is the West Digest. John B. West, founder of West Publishing, developed the West Digest Classification System for the case reporters published as part of the West National Reporter System.[1]

1. Robert M. Jarvis, *John B. West: Founder of the West Publishing Company*, 50 Am. J. Legal Hist. 1 (2008).

The West Digest System consists of multi-volume indexes of case summaries from a specific jurisdiction arranged by subject and date. West publishes separate digests for individual states, groups of states, and jurisdictional categories. The four jurisdictional categories for digests are federal, state, regional, and combined. A federal digest summarizes cases from all federal courts. A state digest summarizes cases from the state courts as well as from federal courts located in that state. A regional digest summarizes state court decisions from the states within the region but does not summarize any federal cases. A combined digest summarizes cases from all state and federal jurisdictions. Thus, North Carolina state cases are indexed in *West's North Carolina Digest, 2d* and the *South Eastern Digest, 2d.*[2] North Carolina federal cases are indexed in *West's North Carolina Digest, 2d* and *West's Federal Practice Digest, 3d.* See Table 8-1 for North Carolina Digests.

Table 8-1. North Carolina Digests

North Carolina Digest	Summaries of cases from North Carolina courts and federal courts in North Carolina.
South Eastern Digest	Summaries of cases from the state courts within the region.
West's Federal Practice Digest	Summaries of cases from United States District Courts, United States Courts of Appeals, and the Supreme Court of the United States.

1. The Organization of the Digest System

The West Digest System is organized around *headnotes* (case summaries) and *Topics and Key Numbers.*

a. Headnotes

As discussed in Chapter 7, each case published in the West National Reporter system has a series of short summary paragraphs corresponding to identified points of law in the case. These paragraphs are located before the text of the

2. A state court case opinion may appear in both a state digest and a regional digest (if available).

actual opinion and are called *headnotes*. The headnotes in the West Reporters are duplicated in the West Digests and are an integral part of the Digest System. West editors then assign each headnote from each case one or more Topic(s) and Key Number(s) from the West Digest System. Each headnote is then added to the digest in the appropriate location under its assigned Topic and Key Number.

b. Topics and Key Numbers and Their Relationship to Headnotes

West *Topics* are the more than 450 subject categories of law originally devised by John West. Topics may be broad subject areas of law, such as "Criminal Law," or narrower subject areas, such as "Good Will." New Topics have been added over the years as new areas of law have developed. West *Key Numbers* are extensive sets of subtopics within each Topic representing every conceivable legal issue under that Topic. Thus, "Wills" Key Number 354 refers to the Topic of "Wills" and the subtopic of "Certificate of Probate." It is important to note that Key Numbers alone, without the Topics, are not helpful, because the same Key Number may be used in many Topics. For example, while Key Number 354 represents the subtopic "Certificate of Probate" under the Topic "Wills," it represents the subtopic "Nature of child custody proceedings" under the Topic "Child Custody."

When you find a relevant Topic and Key Number, you will find right beneath it all the headnotes from all the cases that address that legal issue in that jurisdiction. Under each Topic and Key Number, the headnotes are listed in the hierarchical order of the courts in that jurisdiction. For example, in the *North Carolina Digest*, cases from the North Carolina Supreme Court are listed first, then cases from the North Carolina Court of Appeals. Each headnote listed in the digest includes a case name and reporter citation, allowing you to easily move from the headnotes in the digest to the reporter (print or online) using the citation. See Figure 8-1 for an example of a page from the *North Carolina Digest*.

One of the many useful features of the West Digest System is that the Topics and Key Numbers are consistent throughout all jurisdictions in the United States. Once you find Topic(s) and Key Number(s) relevant to your research question, you can go to the digest for any jurisdiction, state or federal, and find cases addressing that question.

Figure 8-1. Example from West's *North Carolina* Digest

⊂=400 CHILD CUSTODY 6A N C D 2d—206

For later cases, see same Topic and Key Number in Pocket Part

suit to adjudicate "status" is in rem proceeding. G.S. § 1–75.3(c).
In re Trueman, 393 S.E.2d 569, 99 N.C.App. 579.

N.C.App. 1983. Matters of custody, which include visitation rights, are pending until death of one of the parties or the child reaches age of majority. G.S. § 50A–2(2).
Beck v. Beck, 306 S.E.2d 580, 64 N.C.App. 89.

N.C.App. 1978. Generally speaking, actions for child custody, child support and alimony follow the same procedures as other civil actions. G.S. §§ 50–13.5(a, f), 50–16.8(a); Rules of Civil Procedure, rule 3, G.S. § 1A–1.
Benson v. Benson, 249 S.E.2d 877, 39 N.C.App. 254.

N.C.App. 1968. After final judgment of previously instituted divorce action in which custody and support had not been brought to issue or determined, the custody and support issue might be determined in an independent action in another court. G.S. §§ 1–410(5), 50–13.1 et seq., 50–13.5(b)(2), (f).
In re Holt, 160 S.E.2d 90, 1 N.C.App. 108.

⊂=401. Nature of child custody proceedings.

N.C. 1964. When wife has instituted action upon proper allegations for alimony without divorce, she may in original complaint or either party may by motion seek determination of custody of children of marriage and order for support of such children even if it be determined that wife is not entitled to alimony, but action for custody and support may not be maintained under statute providing for alimony without divorce in absence of claim, upon proper allegations, of alimony by wife. G.S. §§ 50-13, 50-16.
Murphy v. Murphy, 134 S.E.2d 148, 261 N.C. 95.

N.C. 1948. Divorce action as it relates to custody of minor children is in the nature of an in rem proceeding and court must have jurisdiction over the children before it can enter a valid order respecting their custody. G.S. § 50–13.
Coble v. Coble, 47 S.E.2d 798, 229 N.C. 81.

N.C.App. 2013. Adoption proceedings and custody proceedings present the same fundamental question, asking who has the right to legal and physical custody of the minor child. West's N.C.G.S.A. §§ 48–1–106(a), 50–13.1.
Johns v. Welker, 744 S.E.2d 486.

N.C.App. 1971. It was proper to seek custody and support of minor child in action for divorce from bed and board. G.S. §§ 50–13.4(b, e), 50–13.5(b) (3), 50–16.7(a), 50–16.8(f); Rules of Civil Procedure, rule 52, G.S. § 1A–1.
Peoples v. Peoples, 179 S.E.2d 138, 10 N.C.App. 402.

⊂=402. Purpose of proceedings.

N.C.App. 1969. Evidence of adulterous conduct, like evidence of other conduct, is relevant upon an inquiry of fitness of a person for purpose of awarding custody of minor children to him or to her, but in a custody proceeding it is not the court's function to punish or reward a parent by withholding or awarding custody of minor children; the court's function in such a proceeding is to diligently seek to act for best interests and welfare of the minor children.
In re McCraw Children, 165 S.E.2d 1, 3 N.C.App. 390.

⊂=403. Jurisdiction.

⊂=404. —— In general.

N.C. 1974. Court in which a divorce action is brought acquires jurisdiction over the custody of the unemancipated children of the marriage, and such jurisdiction continues even after the divorce becomes final.
Blackley v. Blackley, 204 S.E.2d 678, 285 N.C. 358.

N.C. 1972. After separation followed by action for divorce in which a complaint has been filed or a writ of habeas corpus has issued, authority to provide for custody of children vests in the court in which the divorce proceeding is pending.
Shoaf v. Shoaf, 192 S.E.2d 299, 282 N.C. 287.

N.C. 1968. Generally, the court in which a divorce action is instituted acquires jurisdiction over the custody of unemancipated children of the parties, and

† This Case was not selected for publication in the National Reporter System

Source: West's North Carolina Digest. Reprinted with permission of Thomson Reuters.

2. Using the West Digest System

a. West's Key Number System on Westlaw

Today, most legal research is performed online. Thus, the West Digest System is now available through Westlaw and is an essential component of online researching on Westlaw. When you retrieve a case on Westlaw, it contains the same headnotes that appear in the print version of the case, but they are hyperlinked to the online version of the digest.

Figure 8-2. West Key Number System

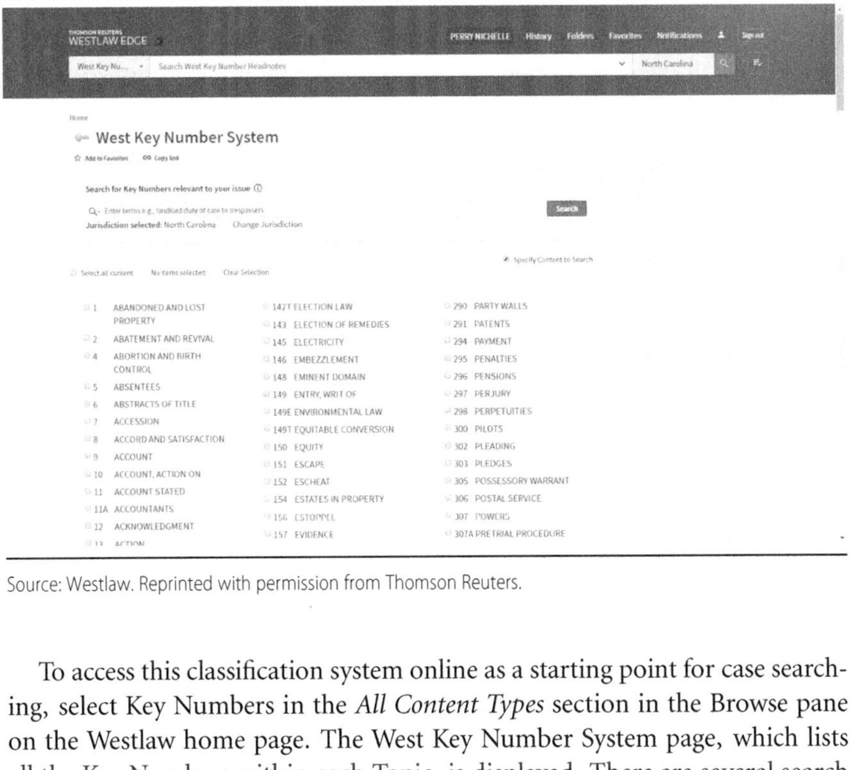

Source: Westlaw. Reprinted with permission from Thomson Reuters.

To access this classification system online as a starting point for case searching, select Key Numbers in the *All Content Types* section in the Browse pane on the Westlaw home page. The West Key Number System page, which lists all the Key Numbers within each Topic, is displayed. There are several search options at this point.

The first option at the Key Number page is to search for Key Numbers relevant to your research question within a jurisdiction. To do this, select a jurisdiction, such as North Carolina, and then enter your search terms in the search bar. This option searches the text of all the Topics and headnotes in the digest of cases from the selected jurisdiction.

The second option is to simply browse the Topics and Key Numbers looking for relevant cases. This option allows you to browse all 400+ Topics, broken out by Key Number headings and eventually by headnotes, and then view individual cases under a specific Key Number. See Figure 8-2 for a view of browsing the list of Topics and Key Numbers on Westlaw.

Note that on Westlaw, the Topics have also been assigned numbers, which display in the digest list of Topics. A Topic may be represented by either the Topic name or its number before the "K" (or key symbol), and the Key Number follows.

i. Topic and Key Numbers from a Retrieved Case

Another way to access the digest online is to select a Topic and Key Number from a headnote of a retrieved case you located on Westlaw. You will then see a list of all the cases under that Topic and Key Number from that case's jurisdiction.

ii. Using a Topic and Key Number to Create a Search

Using a known Topic and Key Number, you can select any jurisdiction from the universal search bar at the main Westlaw page and enter the Topic and Key Number as a search term without going through the West Key Number System page. As mentioned earlier, Topic names are also assigned a unique number. Using a Topic and Key number as a search term requires that you use the Topic number instead of the Topic name, along with the Key Number. For example, the Topic "Adoption," which is Topic Number 17 on Westlaw, and the subtopic, "Persons who may be adopted," which is Key Number 5, would be entered as 17K5 with no spaces. Westlaw recognizes the number 17 as the Topic "Adoption," and the letter "K" instructs the search software that this is a Topic and Key Number search within the database.

b. Using Print Digests

There are several methods of using the print digest to find cases relevant to a specific topic. Which method is best always depends on what information you already have when approaching the digest.

i. The "One Good Case" Method

Occasionally, you will begin a project with a relevant case already in hand. For example, a more experienced attorney may suggest that you look at the *Smith* case from several years ago before starting your case law research because she thinks it might be relevant to your research question. If the *Smith* case contains a headnote that addresses your legal question, simply note the Topic and Key Number of the headnote. Then, in the digest, skim the other headnotes listed under that Topic and Key Number, which refer to all the relevant cases addressing your legal question in your jurisdiction. This is perhaps the easiest way to use the digest.

ii. Descriptive Word Index Method

Typically, however, you will not be starting with a case already in hand; you may only know the legal question you need to answer. In that situation, the best starting point for finding relevant cases will likely be the Descriptive Word Index. The purpose of the Descriptive Word Index is to connect your search terms to related Topics and Key Numbers in the digest, and more importantly, to the headnotes listed under the Key Numbers.

To use the Descriptive Word Index, you must first generate search terms, as addressed in Chapter 2. Of course, the more specific and relevant your search terms, the easier it will be to connect to relevant Topics and Key Numbers in the digest. Next, search for these terms in the Descriptive Word Index of the digest for the jurisdiction in which your legal question arises. The index is arranged alphabetically. Look up each search term in the index and record the Topics and Key Numbers you find. Be sure to check the pocket part of each volume of the Descriptive Word Index.

If you encounter challenges finding cases using your search terms, return to one or more secondary sources, such as a legal encyclopedia, a subject-specific treatise, or a law review or journal article, to get more background information about the legal question you are researching. This approach will help you refine your search terms, resulting in a more productive Descriptive Word Index search.

The next step is to move from the Descriptive Word Index to the main volumes of the digest to begin checking the specific Topics and Key Numbers you identified as relevant. The Topics are printed on the spine of the volumes and are arranged throughout the digest set in alphabetical order. Select the volume containing your Topic, then locate your Topic. Sometimes it is helpful to quickly browse the information at the beginning of your Topic to see what other legal issues are covered under that Topic. It may also be helpful to consult the section called "Subjects Excluded and Covered by Other Topics."

Under your Topic heading you will find a table of contents listing all the Key Numbers for that Topic, referred to as "Analysis" or "Topic Analysis." If there are many Key Numbers, there may be a summary table of contents preceding the more detailed table of contents that includes all the Key Numbers. You may benefit from browsing the Analysis to see where the Key Numbers you identified from the Descriptive Word Index fit within the larger framework of the Topic. You may even find additional relevant Key Numbers as you are browsing.

Next, locate each Key Number you identified in the Descriptive Word Index and read the case headnotes. Record the names and citations of any cases that seem relevant and worth reading based upon your review of the headnotes. Although this process might seem repetitive, dull, or monotonous, it is critically important to the outcome of your research. Careful and thorough review of the Key Numbers and headnotes will give you more confidence later, when you begin to draw conclusions from your research.

The next step in researching case law using print digests is to update the information you found in the Topic volume. This process has several layers: (1)

checking the same Topic and Key Numbers in the volume's pocket part; (2) consulting a free-standing paperback supplement to the volume, usually housed adjacent to the volume; and (3) searching for a cumulative supplementary pamphlet for the full digest (usually published quarterly or semi-annually). These pamphlets are usually shelved at the end of the digest set and should be checked if available. The outside cover of each pamphlet notes the applicable coverage dates.[3]

iii. Topic Analysis or Outline Method

When you have researched a legal question numerous times, or have developed a sophisticated understanding of how to use a digest, you may want to try the "Topic Analysis Method" or "Outline Approach." This approach involves selecting the appropriate Topic volume from the shelf (bypassing the Descriptive Word Index) and examining the Topic Analysis or Outline to find relevant Key Numbers. If you practice criminal law, for example, and you have routinely used the digest to find case law, you might be in a position to work directly from the "Criminal Law" Topic.

The danger of this method is that you might entirely miss non-intuitive Topics that contain relevant Key Numbers. The Descriptive Word Index is designed to prevent that from happening.

iv. Table of Cases Method

Occasionally, you know the name of one or both parties to a relevant case (plaintiff or defendant) but not the citation. The Table of Cases at the end of each digest set provides a list of all the cases in that digest arranged alphabetically by plaintiff and defendant. Using the "Table of Cases" might facilitate the "One Good Case" method described above.

---

3. Even the cumulative supplementary pamphlets may need to be updated. Locate the "most recent case included in this pamphlet" information from the cumulative supplementary pamphlet. This will tell you the volume and page number of the reporter containing the last case included in the cumulative supplementary pamphlet. Recall that each reporter volume of any West reporter set, such as the *South Eastern Reporter*, includes a miniature digest of the cases included in the volume. Find the reporter volume identified by the cumulative supplementary pamphlet and look up your Topic and Key Numbers in that individual volume's digest to find any relevant cases in that volume. Do this for each subsequent volume. Then, follow this same procedure for each advance sheet pamphlet issued for that reporter set. This process will ultimately bring you up to approximately several weeks from the present time. To be more current beyond the most recent advance sheet digests, you must go online.

An alternative use of the Table of Cases is to transition from a reported case that lacks the West Topic and Key Numbers, such as a case in the *North Carolina Supreme Court Reports*, to a West digest, such as the *North Carolina Digest*. You can look up the case in the Table of Cases of the *North Carolina Digest*, using the case name, and find the Topics and Key Numbers associated with that case. From the Table of Cases, you can move to the Topic volume to find relevant headnotes from similar cases under the Key Number(s).

v. Words and Phrases Method

Words that have been judicially defined, and the cases defining them, may be found for a specific jurisdiction using the Words and Phrases part of the digest. A judicially defined word or phrase may be useful when researching a common law issue or an issue governed by a statute that does not have a definitions section. A judicial definition of a term is superior to a generic legal dictionary definition, since the judicial definition is more specific to the relevant jurisdiction. Another useful feature of a Words and Phrases entry is a list of the relevant Topics and Key Numbers assigned to the headnotes in the case that defined the term.

B. Other Online Subject-Based Search Methods

1. Westlaw's Practice Areas

Another method of subject searching on Westlaw is selecting a database that has already been limited to cases concerning a particular subject. One of the best practices when you are full-text keyword searching is to begin with the smallest database that is likely to have all the relevant cases.

Westlaw has made this easy for you by creating Westlaw Practice Area searching. Developed Practice Areas include criminal law, family law, and workers' compensation. From the main Westlaw screen, select the "Practice areas" tab below the universal search bar. In addition to state cases in each topical area, these databases contain other helpful information and research leads; for example, category pages generally contain references to treatises, forms, journals, federal materials, and international materials covering all aspects of a subject area.

2. Lexis

a. "Browse Topics" Find and Search by Legal Topic

Lexis provides searching by subject, or more precisely, searching for relevant cases in databases containing cases already identified by Lexis as focusing on specific areas of law. The Browse feature allows you to search for cases utilizing

Figure 8-3. Lexis "Practice Areas and Topics" Page

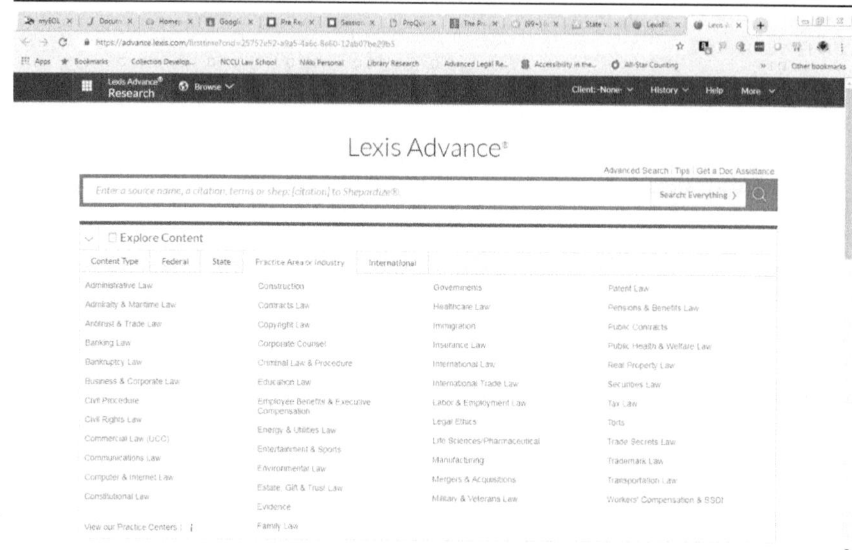

Source: Lexis Advance. Reprinted with the permission of LexisNexis.

the Lexis topical hierarchy. On the Lexis homepage, click Browse above the universal search bar, then select "Topics." You can search for specific topics or browse the levels of the Topic hierarchy.

b. Browse Practice Centers

An easier but slightly broader approach to topic searching in Lexis is to select the "Practice Area and Industry" link just below the universal search bar on the main page. This selection presents you with the top-level Topic Index of over forty topics. Choosing one or more of these topics will add a database of pre-identified cases relating to those topics to the content that is searched from the universal search bar. See Figure 8-3 for an example of a Lexis "Practice Areas and Topics" page.

c. Working from Lexis Headnotes

Another way to find relevant cases is to use the "one good case" method. While examining the full text of a relevant case, identify the relevant headnotes from the beginning of the case and select the subtopics listed in the headnote(s). Clicking on one of these headings and then clicking on "Get Documents" will lead you to a list of other cases assigned to the same topic. This is similar to selecting the Topic and Key Numbers from headnotes in relevant cases while

Figure 8-4. Lexis Document: Anderson v. Liberty Lobby, Inc., 477 U.S. 242

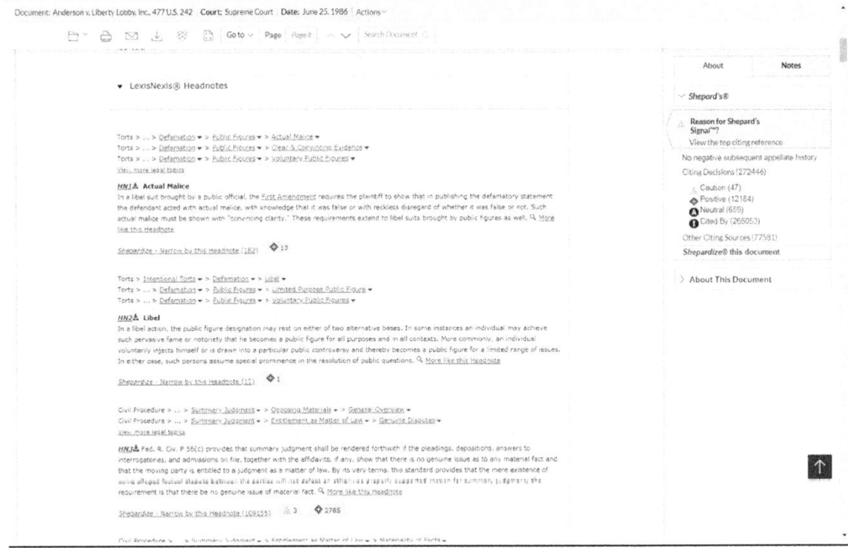

Source: Lexis Advance. Reprinted with the permission of LexisNexis.

using Westlaw.[4] See Figure 8-4 for an example of subtopics in headnotes from a case in Lexis.

3. Topic Searching in Bloomberg

The easiest way to search by topic in Bloomberg is to use Bloomberg Law Practice Centers. Each Practice Center features resources from the entirety of Bloomberg, including Agency Materials, Federal Documents, Federal Opinions, From the Editor, Laws & Regulations, Legal Analysis, News, Practical Guidance, Practice Tools, State Rules, and Specialized Subjects. Bloomberg currently provides fifteen practice Centers: Antitrust, Banking & Finance, Bankruptcy, Benefits & Executive Compensation, Corporate, E-Discovery, Environmental & Safety, Health, Labor & Employment, Patent & Trade Secrets, Privacy & Data Security, Securities, Tax, Tech & Telecom, and Trademark & Copyrights.

4. Lexis headnotes are a little different from Westlaw headnotes. Lexis headnotes are still organized by broad topics and then progressively subdivided by narrower subjects, but Lexis headnote subjects tend to be broader concepts than the West Key Numbers. Also, Lexis headnotes do not editorialize, they use actual language directly from the text of the case.

Figure 8-5. The E-Discovery Practice Center Page in Bloomberg Law

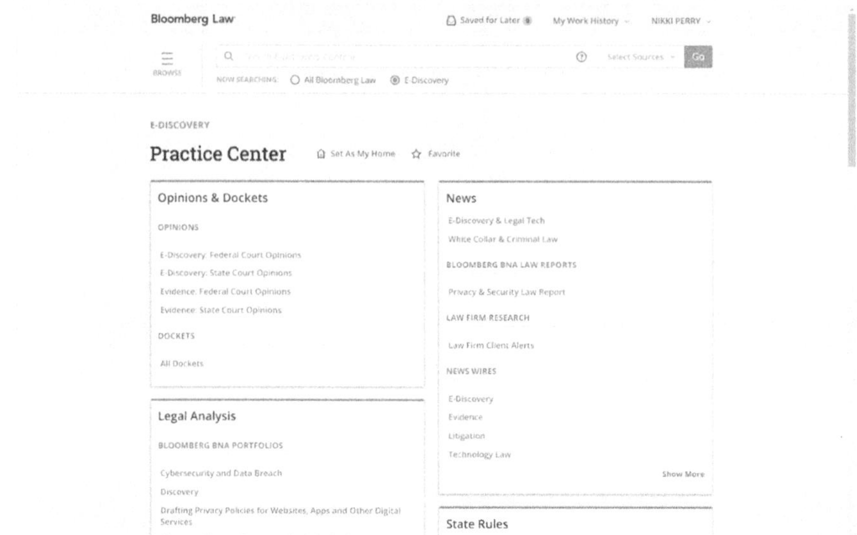

Source: Bloomberg Law. Used with permission of Bloomberg Law.

To access the Practice Centers, click the Browse All Content icon, and from the drop-down menu, select Practice Centers. Within each Center, using the link to "Opinions and Dockets," you have a number of ways to browse and search a subset of cases that Bloomberg has already identified as topic-relevant. For example, see Figure 8-5 to view the "E-Discovery Practice Center" page from Bloomberg.

II. Updating Cases

As we mentioned in Chapter 2, the most effective way to update your research is to use a citator. Citators indicate how an authority has been treated by later actions of a court, legislature, or agency. A citator tells you whether subsequent authorities still follow the authority you have located or have reversed, overruled, or criticized it.

A. Citators for Case Law

In North Carolina, as in the rest of the United States, online citators are the preferred method of updating case law because they are easy to use and very current.[5] KeyCite on Westlaw, Shepard's on Lexis, and BCite on Bloomberg all provide citator information.

KeyCite, Shepard's, and BCite share some common features. First, important terminology is similar. When updating a case, the case being updated is called the *cited case*. All of the citations listed by the citator are documents that cite the cited case. All of the documents listed in the citator as citing the cited case are called *citing sources*. The process of updating involves examining each of the citing sources to see how they treat the cited case. KeyCite, Shepard's, and BCite provide editorial enhancements for some of the citing sources suggesting how they treat the cited case. All three systems allow you to narrow the list of citing sources by jurisdiction, and KeyCite and Shepard's allow you to narrow the list by point of law in the cited case.

Color-coded symbols suggest how the citing case treats the cited case. Just as you should not rely solely on headnotes to explain how legal issues are dealt with in a case without reading the text of that case, you should not rely solely on the color-coded symbols to indicate how a citing source treats a cited source. The assignment of the symbols depends on an editor's interpretation of the issues and outcome in each case. While there are editorial safeguards in place to prevent error, human error or legitimate difference of opinion is always possible. Additionally, since there are often multiple legal issues in a case, a symbol assigned to a case might reference a part of the case not relevant to your research. You should examine each relevant citing source to determine for yourself what effect it has on the reliability of the cited case, using the symbols only to prioritize the order in which you will examine the citing sources. The color-coded symbols for each service are described in Tables 8-2, 8-3, and 8-4 later in this chapter.

---

5. Online citators are typically updated within 24–48 hours of the creation of new information about a case. Because of their superiority as research tools, this chapter will focus on the use of online citators. Note that Shepard's remains available as a print publication. Researchers in North Carolina may use *Shepard's North Carolina Citations*, which lists authorities citing each case published *in North Carolina Reports, North Carolina Court of Appeals Reports*, and *West's South Eastern Reporter*. Another Shepard's set, *Shepard's South Eastern Reporter Citations*, provide lists of cases citing each case published in the *South Eastern Reporter*. Although not complex, the use of Shepard's in print is cumbersome and the information is limited in time by the printing and distribution process. The most current information available in print might still be two to four weeks old. If you are ever faced with using Shepard's in print, consult the detailed instructions included in the "Guide to Shepard's" section in the softbound supplements.

1. Updating Cases Using Shepard's on Lexis

There are several ways to Shepardize a case on Lexis. Once a case is retrieved and displayed on the screen, select the "Shepardize" button or click the signal near the case name. Shepard's will then produce a citation report for that case. Alternatively, if you already have a case citation, and you do not need to view the text of the case in Lexis first, simply type "Shep" followed by the citation into the universal search bar.

a. The Shepard's Display

The Shepard's display defaults to the list view of the appellate history portion of the Shepard's report. This section provides the subsequent history of the cited case. To view this information in an interactive visual format, click the "Map" button. With complex litigation, the visual presentation can answer many questions and make the flow of litigation in the cited case more understandable. The case names in the chart are linked to the full text of the decisions, just as they would be in a citation list.

To view all citing sources for the cited case, click on the "Citing Decisions" section. This section provides a list of every source in the Lexis system that cites the cited case. By default, the sources are listed by jurisdiction, with the most recent sources first. To change the order, use the "Sort by" drop-down menu. The other "sort by" categories include analysis, discussion (how much the citing source discusses the cited case), court, and date. You can also change the order by using the "Sort by" drop-down menu.

Sorting by the "Analysis" link will bring sources with negative analysis to the top. Lexis editors label each source with an analysis label to indicate how it treats the cited case. These include negative labels such as "criticized" or "distinguished," positive labels such as "followed," and neutral labels such as "explained," "harmonized," or "cited in a concurring or dissenting opinion." See Figure 8-6 for an example of the "Citing Decisions" tab display of a Shepard's report on Lexis for the North Carolina Court of Appeals decision in *Cody v. Snider Lumber Co.*, 96 N.C. App. 293, 385 S.E.2d 515 (1989).

b. The Meaning and Use of the Citator Symbols

Shepard's employs a number of symbols to express the editors' judgment about the value of a cited case, so that you can quickly make a reasonable assessment of whether that case is still good law. In addition, the editors assess the value of each citing source and assign symbols. These symbols should be used cautiously, and you should read the text of the citing sources to make your own assessment. The real value in using the symbols is to help you pri-

Figure 8-6. Shepard's Citing Decisions Tab

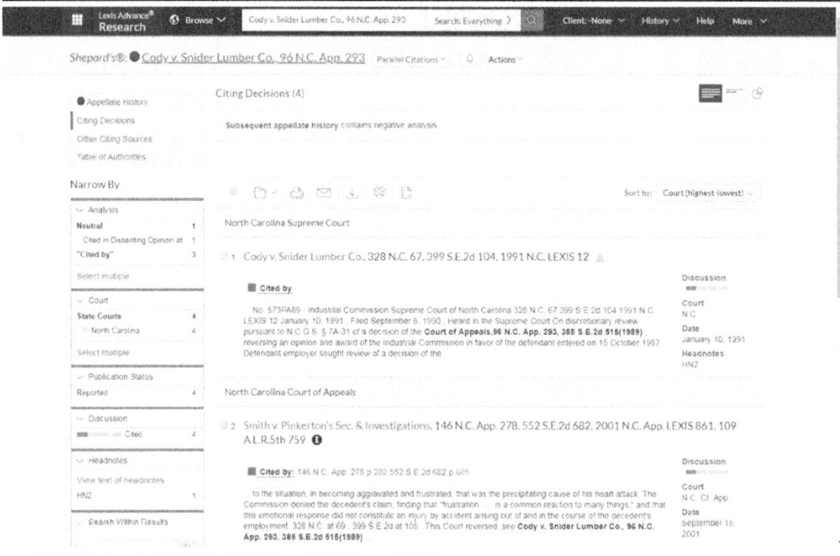

Source: Lexis Advance. Reprinted with the permission of LexisNexis.

oritize the order in which you read the citing sources. Table 8-2 lists and defines the Shepard's symbols.

Table 8-2. Symbols for Updating with Shepard's

Red "Stop" Sign	The editors have identified strong negative treatment for at least one legal issue in the cited case. At least one part of the case may possibly have been overturned or reversed.
Orange "Q"	The editors found at least one citing source that questions one of the legal issues in the cited case, which might affect its precedential value.
Yellow Triangle	The handling of at least one legal issue in the cited case has been criticized by or distinguished by another source.
Blue "I"	One or more sources cite the cited case without giving it any treatment.
Blue "A"	The editors found at least citing source that addresses the cited source, but that treatment is neutral. For example, the citing source may explain the cited case without stating a positive or negative interpretation.
Green "+" Sign	There is only positive treatment for the cited case, such as "affirmed" or "follow by."

The symbols may appear in several places within the report. The most important symbol is the one at the top of the screen next to the name of the cited case. You can scroll over the symbol for a quick reminder of the symbol's meaning. Alternatively, Shepard's provides a signal legend at the top right of the screen. Citing sources may also have symbols beside them, indicating the strength of each of those sources. While that could be important if a source treating the cited case negatively was later reversed or overruled, usually you are mostly interested in the symbol applied to the cited case at the top of the screen. The significance of these two different placements of the symbols should not be confused.

The "Other Citing Sources" section provides a list of all other sources (Treatises, Statutes, Regulations) on Lexis that cite the cited case. The "Table of Authorities" section lists all the sources cited within the cited case along with an analysis status and a status symbol for those cases. Although not a substitute for a thorough reading of these sources, this list can give you a quick indication of the overall status of the authority on which the cited case relies.

c. Narrowing the Citing Documents with Shepard's

For cases that have been frequently cited and thus have a lengthy citation report, you may find it useful to limit the type of information included in the report. An extreme example is *Roe v. Wade*, 410 U.S. 113 (1973). There are more than 15,000 documents on Lexis citing *Roe v. Wade*. The only reasonable way to begin analyzing that volume of citing sources is to filter them.

Shepard's offers several ways to narrow the results: analysis, court, discussion, headnotes, keyword, and timeline. These categories appear down the left side of the report. See Figure 8-6 above for an example. This feature is responsive, so it will show only the options that exist for the cited case. Table 8-3 outlines the "narrow by results" categories.

Table 8-3. Shepard's "Narrow by Categories"

Analysis	Allows you to view sources that treat the cited case in a particular way. The more negative options appear at the top (assuming the cited case has received any negative treatment).
Court	Allows you to view sources from a particular jurisdiction. This is extremely helpful, especially when you have limited time to spend analyzing the report or when the cited case has been cited extensively. Note that you can select multiple sources at once.
Discussion	Allows you to view only spurces that analyze or discuss the cited case rather than those that simply mention or cite it in passing.
Headnote	Allows you to view sources that cite the cited case for a particular issue or topic. If you do not remember which headnotes are relevant, simply pause your cursor over the headnote number to be reminded of the topic.
Keyword	Allows you to search all the sources listed on the Shepard's report using keywords. A search box is provided in the list of filters.
Timeline	Allows you to view sources within a particular time period. You will see a graph depicting how often the cited case has been cited over time. To narrow the time period, simply type the years into the two boxes and click the "OK" box.

d. Analyzing the Citing Sources' Treatment of the Cited Case

Although the editors provide colorful symbols alerting you to positive and potentially negative treatment of the cited case, it is your ethical and professional responsibility to interpret how the citing sources affect the cited case. The essence of updating with citators is applying your professional judgment to determine how cited source affects the citing case.

Clicking on the name of a citing source in the list takes you to the relevant part of the source that cites and perhaps discusses the cited case. If the pinpointed information about the cited case seems relevant, be sure to read the entire source so that you can understand the pinpointed information in the larger context of the whole citing source.

In addition to positive and negative treatment, you might discover that many citing sources cite the cited case for another point of law and are therefore not relevant to your inquiry. Also, some citing sources may simply cite the cited case without ascribing any meaning or value to it. These citing sources should be disregarded.

Figure 8-7. KeyCite on Westlaw

Source: Westlaw Edge. Reprinted with permission of Thomson Reuters.

Several other benefits may flow from the time and effort you spend updating cases. For example, one of the sources citing the cited case may actually be more factually or legally relevant to your research question. One of the citing sources might also raise additional relevant issues you had not yet considered. Because of these research benefits, it is wise to update cases throughout the research process rather than to wait until the end of the process.

2. Updating Cases Using KeyCite on Westlaw

When a case (or other document) is displayed on Westlaw, KeyCite information is automatically provided in tabs along the top of the screen. See Figure 8-7 for an example of how the information is displayed for the North Carolina case of *Cody v. Snider Lumber Co.*, 96 N.C. App. 293, 385 S.E.2d 515 (1989). The KeyCite status symbol is prominently displayed next to the case name. The tabs along the top of the case text contain links to various parts of the KeyCite report.

a. The KeyCite Display

The "History" tab provides the direct history of the cited case, both prior and subsequent. This list indicates whether the cited case reversed or remanded a lower court's ruling, as well as whether it was appealed and, if so, its disposition on appeal. This information is provided in both a list and graphic form. When the cited case was part of complex litigation, the graphic presentation can help you understand the flow of litigation in the case. The case names in the chart are linked to the full text of the decisions, just as they are in the list.

The "Negative Treatment" tab presents any negative direct history followed by citing sources that treat the cited case negatively. This list includes sources that overrule, criticize, distinguish, modify or call into doubt the cited case. The sources are organized by treatment (with the most negative listed first) and then by jurisdiction in reverse chronological order. You cannot re-sort or filter the order of the sources with this tab. To use that functionality, click over to the "Citing References" tab.

The "Citing References" tab lists all of the sources that cite the cited case. The default order starts with sources that have the fullest discussion of the cited case, with negative sources always listed first. This order can be changed to sort by date, using the "Sort By" link at the top of the page. KeyCite uses depth of treatment bars to denote the extent to which the citing sources analyze the cited case. Citing sources examining the cited case in the greatest depth are presented first, and those mentioning the cited case only briefly are at the bottom of the list. See Table 8-4 for an explanation of the symbols used.

The "Table of Authorities" tab lists all sources that are cited by the cited case, along with status flags for those sources, giving you a quick indication of the overall status of the authority on which the cited case relies. Remember that skimming this list is not a substitute for reading sources yourself.

Table 8-4. KeyCite Depth of Treatment Symbols

Four Bars	Examined in depth, often more than a full printed page of text.
Three Bars	Discussed less extensively, typically more than a paragraph but less than a printed page.
Two Bars	Cited but little discussion, usually less than a paragraph.
One Bar	Mentioned insignificantly, often in a string citation.
" "	Quotation marks suggest that the citing source includes a direct quotation from the cited case.

b. The Meaning and Use of the KeyCite Status Flags

Just as Shepard's on Lexis assigns symbols such as a red stop sign or a yellow triangle to sources to denote how they have been treated by subsequent sources, KeyCite uses flags for the same purpose. When KeyCiting a case on Westlaw, always look for a KeyCite status flag next to the case name. The status flag is a quick reference symbol indicating the editors' opinion about whether the cited case is still "good law." Although it should not be relied upon as authoritative, this quick indication of the strength of the cited case can be useful for prioritizing your research and delving into your own inquiry about the strength of the cited case. See Table 8-5 for a list of the KeyCite status flags and a brief description of their meaning.

Table 8-5. KeyCite Status Indicators

Red Flag	The editors discovered strong negative treatment, such as the cited case being reversed on appeal or overturned by another source, and determined it is no longer "good law" for at least one legal point.
Yellow Flag	The editors found some negative treatment, but the cited case has not been reversed or overturned.
Orange Triangle	The editors determined that there is a risk that the cited case may no longer be good for at least one point of law based on its reliance on an overruled or otherwise invalid prior decision.

c. Narrowing the Citing Sources with KeyCite

When a case has been cited by many other sources, it may not be realistic to attempt to review each citing source. Recall from the discussion of Shepard's, for example, that *Roe v. Wade* has been cited by an unmanageable number of sources. The same is true for Westlaw's KeyCite. *Roe v. Wade* has over 26,000 citing sources on Westlaw. Due to time constraints, a best practice would be to use the citator service to assist in prioritizing the order in which you will review citing sources. Certainly, those sources suggesting negative treatment should be reviewed first.

Like Shepard's, KeyCite offers ways to limit the citations report to information that is most relevant to your research. On the "Citing References" tab, which lists all sources on Westlaw that cite the cited case, you can view the filtering options in the left margin. This list will differ depending on the characteristics of the citing sources. For example, if no sources cite the cited case,

Figure 8-8. Westlaw KeyCite Filters

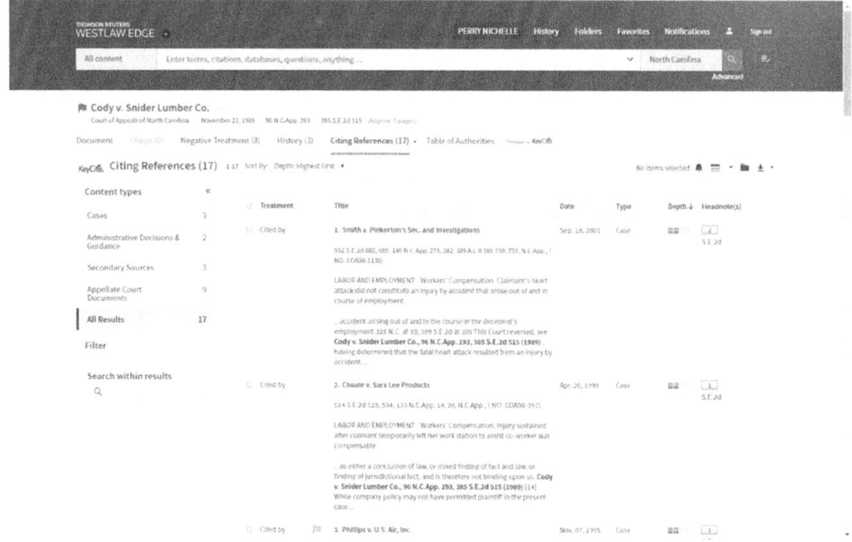

Source: Westlaw Edge. Reprinted with permission of Thomson Reuters.

that filter will not appear in the left margin. Further, if only North Carolina sources cite the cited case, only North Carolina will be listed under the "Jurisdiction" filter.

Potential filters for cases include keyword, jurisdiction, date, depth of treatment, headnote, treatment status, document type, and publication status. These filters function very much like the Shepard's filters described above. If you work with just one filter at a time, KeyCite will automatically apply the filter as you click on the box (e.g., clicking on a particular headnote or depth of treatment). To use more than one filter, click on "Select Multiple Filters." See Figure 8-8 to view the KeyCite case filters available for *Cody v. Snider Lumber Co.*

d. Analyzing the Citing Sources' Treatment of the Cited Case

Again, there is no substitute for examining the citing sources yourself. Certainly, all the citing sources you wish to rely on from the citations report should be closely examined, and the legal issues in each source should be understood within the entire context of that source, not read in isolation.

3. Updating Cases Using BCite on Bloomberg

As a relative newcomer to the legal market, Bloomberg's BCite is the newest citator product. It was developed in the 2000s, when Bloomberg decided to add an editorially created citator to its product. Bloomberg's staff reviewed all of the cases on Bloomberg to create BCite.

When viewing a case on Bloomberg, the BCite symbol appears next to the cited case to indicate the general status of the case. Details appear on the right in the BCite Analysis pane and in the tabs across the top of the document.

The cited case's prior and subsequent history can be viewed by clicking the "Direct History" link or tab. The total number of sources citing the cited case, along with a breakdown by treatment indicator (such as positive, distinguished, or criticized), is shown in the pane to the right of the case text. See Table 8-6 for a list of the possible BCite indicators.

Table 8-6. BCite Indicators

Green Plus Sign	Positive. The editors found no citing sources or found sources that follow or discuss the cited case with approval.
Blue Checkmark	Distinguished. The editors determined that at least one source distinguished the case on the facts or the law.
Yellow Triangle	Caution. The editors discovered either a sources in the direct history that modified or clarified the cited case or a source that criticized the cited case's legal reasoning without directly overruling it.
Orange Circle	Superseded by statute. The editors decided that at least one source has affirmatively stated that the cited case has been rendered obsolete, displaced, or superseded by a statute or regulation.
Red Minus Sign	Negative. The editors determined that at least part of the cited case was reversed, vacated, or depublished in full or in part by a case in its direct history, at least part of the case has been overruled by any court.
Grey X	Pending. Bloomberg Law editors are reviewing the case.

To view all of the sources that cite the cited case, click the "Case Analysis" link. By default, this list is in pure chronological order, but it can be changed to sort by most cited cases (called citation frequency), by citing source analysis (which brings the most negative treatment to the top), or by court. BCite also offers a number of filters that can be used to limit the results: analysis, status, citation frequency, court, judge, and date. The "analysis" filter allows you to see sources that have treated the cited case in a particular way, such as "criticized" or "distinguished." The "status" filter allows you to see sources with a particular status (such as negative). Note that there is not a way to limit the results by topic or subject on this tab. There is a topic filter for sources, though, on the "Citing Documents" tab.

The "Citing Documents" tab provides a list of all sources on Bloomberg that cite the cited case, including court opinions. You can filter the results by type of document and date. Once you have filtered by type of document, additional filters may be available. For example, the "court opinions" filter allows you to filter by the topic of the citing source.

The "Table of Authorities" tab lists the sources cited within the cited case and indicates how these sources were treated by the cited case and the general status symbol for each source, quickly suggesting the overall status of the authorities on which the cited case relies.

4. Prioritizing Citing Sources

Regardless of the citator system used, the best practice is not to rely fully on a publisher's editorial judgment or opinions. When you do not have time to read and examine all the cases in a citing list, you must use your professional judgment to determine the best use of your time when fulfilling your ethical and professional obligation to your client or the person for whom you are researching. Consider some of the following issues when prioritizing which citing sources to read within a restricted time frame.

- Indications of negative treatment should be given highest priority. It is critical to know of any subsequent appeal of the cited case resulting in a reversal. Other citing sources that the editors believe have overruled, criticized, or even simply distinguished the cited case should be closely evaluated.
- Consider limiting the citing sources to those within your jurisdiction, since you are mainly interested in primary mandatory authority. This strategy works particularly well for federal cases; it might be less useful when updating North Carolina cases, since most of the citing sources will be from North Carolina.
- Consider prioritizing your reading and analysis by court hierarchy. Shepard's arranges citing sources in hierarchical order by highest court. KeyCite lists citing sources by depth of treatment, but the list can be limited to only the decisions from the highest court within each juris-

diction. The BCite list is presented in pure chronological order, so you should use the filters to prioritize sources in your jurisdiction.

- Consider limiting the citing sources by date so that you can read the most recent sources first.
- Consider using headnotes to limit the citing sources. If a source deals with multiple topics, you may be interested in it only for one topic. Limiting citing sources to those whose headnotes discuss the issue in which you are interested will provide the most relevant results. Although BCite does allow filtering by general topic, it does not allow filtering by specific point of law.

III. Tools for the Toolbox

1. The digest system, in print or on Westlaw, is one of the most effective tools for locating cases by subject.
2. Westlaw, Lexis, and Bloomberg all have keyword search options for locating cases.
3. Always use a citator to make sure the case you have found is still good law and to be aware of how other sources have trusted the relevant points of law.

Chapter Nine

Researching Court Rules and Other Practice Rules

In this chapter, we explain how to locate the various rules that help attorneys in the practice of law. They include procedural, evidentiary, and appellate court rules; rules of ethics and professional conduct; and attorney general opinions. Practicing law competently and ethically would be much harder, if not impossible, without these rules. To act in her client's best interests, a practicing attorney must understand and be able to reconcile a body of substantive, procedural, and ethical rules. To do so, she must be able to efficiently access all of those rules. In addition, attorney general opinions give advisory information on issues that may be a bit obscure but are important in specialized areas of practice.

This chapter first discusses how to research court rules that govern attorneys practicing in North Carolina state courts. It then discusses how to research North Carolina rules governing ethics and professionalism. Next, it discusses how to research North Carolina Attorney General opinions. Finally, it discusses how to research the corresponding federal rules and federal attorney general opinions.

I. Rules Governing North Carolina Court Practice

The North Carolina Constitution gives the North Carolina Supreme Court alone the authority to draft and adopt rules of procedure and practice for the appellate courts.[1] The North Carolina General Assembly is vested with the authority to make the rules of procedure and practice for the trial courts. The

1. N.C. Const. art. 4, § 13(2).

General Assembly has delegated this authority to the Supreme Court but has retained the constitutional right to alter, amend, or repeal any rule of procedure or practice adopted by the Supreme Court for the Superior or District Court Divisions.[2] Generally, despite that retained right, the creation and adoption of the rules of the practice of law in North Carolina is in the purview of the Supreme Court.

The most commonly consulted rules are the Rules of Civil Procedure (the rules that specify the procedures that govern civil cases before North Carolina state courts): the Rules of Evidence (the rules that govern what material and testimony can be introduced in courts), and the Rules of Appellate Procedure. Some research questions can be answered by quick reference to the actual text of the rules without the clutter of annotations. The annotated versions of these rules may be more useful for researchers looking for the drafting committee's notes explaining the committee's actions, or summaries of cases interpreting each rule. Some useful research strategies for a selected group of court rules are described below.

A. North Carolina Rules of Civil Procedure

Chapter 1A of the North Carolina General Statutes contains the North Carolina Rules of Civil Procedure. The two annotated versions—the *General Statutes of North Carolina Annotated* and *West's North Carolina General Statutes Annotated*—have the best combination of stability, accessibility, annotations, and indexing. The annotated Rules can be accessed either in print or online on Westlaw and Lexis. They are also available for free on the North Carolina General Statutes page of the General Assembly website, but this source is updated less frequently and does not include annotations.[3]

In addition to these state-wide Rules of Civil Procedure, which apply to every Superior and District Court in North Carolina, many courts have their own local rules. Local rules may address such matters as arguing motions, conducting pre-trial or settlement conferences, conducting discovery, and calendaring matters for hearings. The North Carolina Judicial Branch (formerly the Administrative Office of the Courts) has a web page containing local rules and forms organized by county.[4]

---

2. *Id.*; N.C. Gen. Stat. § 7A-34 (2017).
3. ncleg.net.
4. nccourts.org/Courts/CRS/Policies/LocA.L.R.ules/Default.asp.

B. North Carolina Rules of Evidence

Both *West's North Carolina General Statutes Annotated* and Lexis's *General Statutes of North Carolina Annotated* are excellent sources for an authoritative, annotated version of the North Carolina Rules of Evidence. The Rules of Evidence are incorporated into Chapter 8C of the General Statutes. The rules are annotated in the Lexis print and online versions, but not in the West print or online versions. A free, unannotated version of the North Carolina Rules of Evidence is also available on the General Assembly website.[5]

C. North Carolina Rules of Appellate Procedure

The North Carolina Rules of Appellate Procedure are contained in the *Annotated Rules of North Carolina* annual volume of Lexis's print version of the *General Statutes of North Carolina Annotated.* This annotated version of the Rules is also available on Lexis in the North Carolina State and Federal Court Rules database, where it is searchable and browsable.

Additionally, *West's North Carolina General Statutes Annotated* includes a useful, annotated set of the Rules of Appellate Procedure. Westlaw provides the Rules in a searchable and browsable database called North Carolina Rules of Appellate Procedure. These rules are not annotated, but there is a list of all sources that cite each rule on the Citing References tab. The rules are currently up to date on Westlaw.

The most convenient access to the Rules of Appellate Procedure is through the North Carolina Judicial Branch "Rules" website.[6] There, you will find a free, relatively recent copy of the Rules of Appellate Procedure in PDF format, with any recent amendments separately posted. Significantly, however, the version of the rules on the Judicial Branch website is not annotated and is not as current as the updated versions of the rules on Westlaw and Lexis.

D. Combined Sources

In addition to the separate sources containing these three sets of rules, several sources combine two or more of them into single collections. For example, each year West publishes the *North Carolina Rules of Court-State and Federal.* While convenient, this three-volume softbound set is unannotated.

5. ncleg.net/EnactedLegislation/Statutes/PDF/ByChapter/Chapter_8C.pdf.
6. nccourts.gov/courts/supreme-court/court-rules.

In addition to the rules mentioned above, this collection includes other rules of procedure, such as local court rules, the North Carolina Child Support Guidelines, rules for arbitration, and even rules for commissions such as the North Carolina Industrial Commission and the Real Estate Commission.

Lexis's *General Statutes of North Carolina Annotated* (containing the annual *Annotated Rules of North Carolina* volume) is another convenient source of almost fifty sets of state and federal rules governing the practice of law in North Carolina. The set is also browsable on Lexis in the "North Carolina State and Federal Court Rules" database.

Westlaw includes a "North Carolina Rules of Court" database with many of the same rules contained in the West print source described above. Generally, these rules are not annotated. Table 9-1 includes a list of the available electronic sources that include North Carolina practice rules.

Table 9-1. Summary of Available Electronic Sources for North Carolina Practice Rules

Westlaw
westlaw.com

Lexis
LexisAdvance.com

North Carolina General Assembly Website
ncleg.net/gascripts/statutes/Statutes.asp

North Carolina Judicial Branch Website
nccourts.gov/courts/supreme-court/court-rules

II. North Carolina State Bar Rules, Rules of Ethics, and Ethics Opinions

The North Carolina State Bar, established in 1933,[7] has a number of important, specific functions that control, monitor, and support the practice of law in North Carolina. First, the State Bar, through its Board of Law Examiners, is responsible for examining applicants who wish to practice law in North Carolina and developing and administering the North Carolina Bar Exam. Second,

7. 1933 N.C. Sess. Laws 313 (Chapter 210). The North Carolina Supreme Court approved the Certificate of Organization of the North Carolina State Bar in October 1933; *see* 205 N.C. 853 (1933).

the State Bar requires licensed attorneys to attend continuing legal education (CLE) classes each year and report their attendance, to ensure they stay informed of current legal developments.[8] Third, the State Bar provides standards for specialty certification in several areas of law.

Fourth, the State Bar develops ethics rules, counsels lawyers individually as well as through the issuance of opinions, and provides attorney ethics training events. Finally, the State Bar investigates complaints of attorney misconduct and, if appropriate, conducts disciplinary hearings and imposes sanctions. All of these activities, as well as the general operation of the State Bar organization, require rules for their fair and equitable administration.

A. Rules and Regulations for the North Carolina State Bar

Although privately funded through dues, the State Bar is an agency of the State of North Carolina. The rules governing the State Bar—its organization, operation, and activities—are the "Rules and Regulations for the North Carolina State Bar" (also called the "Administrative Rules of the State Bar") and are codified in Title 27, chapter 1 of the *North Carolina Administrative Code* (N.C.A.C.). Because these rules are part of the N.C.A.C., the information in Chapter 6 about researching in the N.C.A.C. is also relevant to researching State Bar rules.

The State Bar has an excellent website that provides free and convenient access to the Rules and Regulations for the North Carolina State Bar.[9] At this writing, the link for these Rules is available under the "For Lawyers" tab in the top center of the homepage.

The Rules and Regulations for the North Carolina State Bar are also available from several other print sources. The annual *Annotated Rules of North Carolina* volume of Lexis's *General Statutes of North Carolina Annotated* includes the Rules. In addition, West's three-volume softbound set of *North Carolina Rules of Court-State and Federal*, contains the Rules in a convenient desktop version.

B. 2003 Revised Rules of Professional Conduct

Separate and apart from the Rules and Regulations for the North Carolina State Bar described above, the Revised Rules of Professional Conduct govern the ethical practice of law. To be licensed in North Carolina, a person must

8. Continuing legal education materials are covered in Chapter 3.

9. ncbar.gov.

demonstrate her knowledge of these Revised Rules by passing a separate exam, the Multistate Professional Responsibility Exam (MPRE), in addition to the North Carolina Bar Examination. These Revised Rules of Professional Conduct inform the daily practice of law, and all lawyers need to research and consult the Rules periodically to address various ethics issues as they arise.

Like the Rules and Regulations for the North Carolina State Bar, the Revised Rules of Professional Conduct are in Chapter 2, Title 27 of the *North Carolina Administrative Code*. Again, because these Rules are part of the N.C.A.C., the information in Chapter 6 of this book will be most useful for researching these Rules.

The State Bar website provides free and convenient access to the Revised Rules of Professional Conduct under the "For Lawyers" tab in the top center of the homepage.[10] The same print sources that include the Rules and Regulations for the North Carolina State Bar also contain the Revised Rules of Professional Conduct.

C. North Carolina Formal Ethics Opinions

Any member of the North Carolina State Bar may submit a question about legal ethics to the State Bar, by phone or in writing. The State Bar administrative staff sometimes informally answers a phone question immediately. But for questions requiring a written response, the State Bar issues three types of formal written responses: Ethics Opinions, Ethics Decisions, and Ethics Advisories.

Ethics Opinions are the weightiest of the three responses. They are initially considered and proposed by the Ethics Committee of the State Bar; they become Formal Ethics Opinions when they are adopted by the State Bar Council.[11] They represent the State Bar's studied interpretation of the Revised Rules of Professional Conduct applied to a specific fact situation but are considered widely applicable to the Bar membership at large.

Formal Ethics Opinions are most easily found at the North Carolina State Bar website under the "For Lawyers" tab at the top center of the homepage.[12] Formal Ethics Opinions are available back to 1997 and are browsable by citation or title. The Opinions are also keyword searchable. Proposed Opinions are

10. *Id.*

11. For more information about how the State Bar addresses ethics questions, see Chapter 10 of Scott Childs & Nick Sexton, *North Carolina Legal Research Guide* (2d ed. 2009).

12. ncbar.gov.

also posted at the website. Additionally, all of the Formal Ethics Opinions are republished each year in the annual *State Bar Handbook*. Another source for the Opinions is the *State Bar Journal*, which publishes the full text of the proposed Formal Ethics Opinions and then prints a list of the Opinions that are finally adopted. Westlaw and Lexis include databases of North Carolina Formal Ethics Opinions with coverage back to 1986 and 1997, respectively. The coverage on Lexis is a part of the National Reporter on Legal Ethics & Professional Responsibility, which includes only selected opinions.

Earlier selected ethics opinions issued between 1986 and 1997 are also available at the North Carolina State Bar website, although they are organized under a different scheme. Ethics opinions known as "RPCs" were issued under the now superseded (1985) Rules of Professional Conduct. RPCs may still provide guidance on specific ethical issues unless they have been superseded by a subsequent Formal Ethics Opinion or by a provision of the Revised Rules of Professional Conduct. Researchers should review the Revised Rules of Professional Conduct and the Index to Ethics Opinions on the North Carolina State Bar website before relying on an RPC.

D. North Carolina Bar Association

In addition to the State Bar, other organizations support the practice of law in North Carolina. The largest is the North Carolina Bar Association. Unlike the official North Carolina State Bar, the Bar Association is a voluntary organization and does not regulate the practice of law, but it does provide many important benefits to its members. One of those important benefits is free access to an online legal research service called Fastcase. Fastcase provides access to primary law from North Carolina and a number of other states, as well as federal law.

E. North Carolina Attorney General Opinions

In North Carolina, the General Statutes require the Attorney General, who functions as the state's attorney, to issue opinions on questions of law submitted by the General Assembly, the Governor, the Auditor, the Treasurer, or other state officers.[13] Even though Attorney General opinions originate from a branch of the government, they are not primary authority. They are considered advisory only, as they represent the Attorney General's interpretation of the law

13. N.C. Gen. Stat. § 114-2(5) (2017).

applied to a specific question. Courts, however, have found them to be very persuasive if there is no relevant primary authority on a particular point.[14]

The most convenient free option for researching Attorney General Opinions is the North Carolina Department of Justice's website.[15] This searchable and browsable online collection includes opinions issued since 1977. Researchers can also contact the Attorney General's Office directly for copies of opinions that are not available online.

These opinions are also available with similar coverage on Westlaw, Lexis, and Bloomberg. In Westlaw, you can access them by entering "North Carolina Attorney General Opinions" in the universal search bar. In Lexis, you can access the Attorney General Opinions database by selecting "Browse Sources" and then narrowing to North Carolina. On Bloomberg, where coverage of North Carolina Attorney General Opinions begins with December 1955, you can find the database by selecting "All Legal Content" under the "Getting Started" heading, then selecting the "Jurisdiction" tab, narrowing the jurisdiction to North Carolina, and selecting "N.C. Agencies and Departments." Table 9-2 summarizes the steps to finding North Carolina Attorney General Decisions by electronic source.

Table 9-2. Finding North Carolina Attorney General Decisions

Electronic Source	Steps to Find North Carolina Attorney General Opinions
Westlaw	• Enter "North Carolina Attorney General Opinions" in the universal search bar.
Lexis	• Go to the "Browse Sources" link. • Narrow the jurisdiction to North Carolina using the filters in the left margin. • Enter "Attorney General Opinions."
Bloomberg	• Select "All Legal Content" under the "Getting Started" heading. • Select "Jurisdiction" tab. • Narrow the jurisdiction to North Carolina. • Select "N.C. Agencies and Departments."

14. See the North Carolina case, *Lawrence v. Shaw*, stating that Attorney General Opinions are advisory only. *Lawrence v. Shaw*, 210 N.C. 352, 361, 186 S.E. 504, 509 (1936), *rev'd on other grounds*, 300 U.S. 245 (1937).

15. ncdoj.gov/About-DOJ/Legal-Services/Legal-Opinions.aspx.

Law libraries around the state have paper copies of selected Attorney General Opinions with coverage dating at least as far back as 1901. At various periods throughout history, the Opinions have been issued in the *Attorney General Reports*. These paper collections have had various indexing through the years but may be difficult to research. For Opinions issued after 1977, online sources will usually provide better access for researchers, especially for those researching without a citation.

III. Federal Sources of Practitioner Rules

The federal courts most relevant to North Carolina research and practice include the following: the Western, Middle, and Eastern divisions of the United States District Court of North Carolina; the United States Court of Appeals for the Fourth Circuit; and the Supreme Court of the United States. Each of these courts has its own rules of procedure. At the trial level, district courts operate using rules such as the Federal Rules of Civil Procedure, the Federal Rules of Criminal Procedure, and the Federal Rules of Evidence. All of the Courts of Appeals operate under the Federal Rules of Appellate Procedure. The Supreme Court follows its own Rules of the Supreme Court.

A. Federal Rules of Court Procedure/Practice

The United States Courts' "Rules" webpage is an excellent source for federal rules of practice, procedure, and evidence.[16] This site also includes the latest information about pending rule changes and opportunities for comments on proposed rules.

The *United States Code Service* and *United States Code Annotated* are also good sources for federal rules. Both are indexed and annotated, and both are available in the print codes and online at Westlaw and Lexis, respectively. A comprehensive collection of rules appears in volumes at the end of the *United States Code Service* (print version) series. In the *United States Code Annotated* (print version), the Federal Rules of Civil Procedure, the Federal Rules of Evidence, the Federal Rules of Appellate Procedure, and the Rules of the Supreme Court of the United States are included, along with others as an appendix to Title 28. The Federal Rules of Criminal Procedure are part of an appendix to Title 18.

16. U.S.Courts.gov/rules-policies.

The local court rules for each federal court are easily located at each court's website. For example, the local rules for the United States District Court for the Western District of North Carolina can be found online.[17]

Finally, West publishes a three-volume publication called the *North Carolina Rules of Court-State and Federal,* which includes a federal rules volume with federal rules relevant to federal practice in North Carolina. These softbound books are issued each year.

B. The American Bar Association Model Rules of Professional Conduct

Much like the North Carolina Bar Association, the American Bar Association (ABA) is a voluntary organization and does not control the practice of law in any jurisdiction. The ABA, however, has long supported attorney codes of ethics by developing, adopting, and promoting model codes. Currently, the ABA Model Rules of Professional Conduct are used to promote ethical behavior in the legal profession. The Model Rules are available on Westlaw (ABA Annotated Model Rules of Professional Conduct database), Lexis (ABA Model Rules of Professional Conduct and Code of Judicial Conduct database), and Bloomberg (Lawyers' Manual on Professional Conduct: Model Rules and Standards database). While all of the versions include comments from the Model Rules explaining the rules and the reasoning behind their adoption, only the Westlaw version is annotated with cases from jurisdictions that have adopted the rules. Since North Carolina's Revised Rules of Professional Conduct are based upon the ABA Model Rules, the ABA Model Rules are an important source of persuasive authority.

The ABA also issues Formal Ethics Opinions based upon its Model Rules. These Opinions may be persuasive, particularly in jurisdictions that have adopted rules similar to the ABA's Model Rules, as North Carolina has. Many of the Opinions are available at the ABA's Center for Professional Responsibility website for a fee, where the legal researcher may browse a subject index of the Opinions. The Opinions are also available in a searchable database on Lexis. They are not currently available on Westlaw or Bloomberg.

C. U.S. Attorney General Opinions

The Office of the United States Attorney General was created by the Judiciary Act of 1789. The Attorney General is the head of the Justice Department (created in 1870) and serves as the chief law enforcement officer of the

17. ncwd.uscourts.gov.

federal government. Among other duties, the U.S. Attorney General gives advice and issues opinions upon request to the President and the heads of the executive departments of the federal government. The Attorney General has delegated to the U.S. Department of Justice Office of Legal Counsel the duties of providing legal advice to the President and executive branch agencies. These duties include the drafting of the formal Opinions of the Attorney General.

Selected Opinions dating back to 1992 may be found for free at the Office of Legal Counsel website.[18] They are browsable by year. Selected Opinions are also available on Westlaw, Lexis, and Bloomberg. Just as with North Carolina Attorney General Opinions, U.S. Attorney General Opinions are educated interpretations of federal law applied to specific facts;[19] thus, they are not mandatory authority, but they are often persuasive.

IV. Tools for the Toolbox

1. Familiarity with the procedural rules of the trial and appellate courts, both state and Federal, procedural and appellate court rules, rules of evidence, rules of professional conduct, and attorney general opinions is necessary for the effective practice of law.
2. All of these rules may be found in print as well as online.
3. State and local procedural, evidentiary, and appellate rules, as well as their federal equivalents, may be found at the court websites of their respective jurisdictions.
4. North Carolina ethics rules may be found at the State Bar website (www.ncbar.gov) and are free, whereas the Model Rules of Professional Conduct are offered for a fee on the ABA website.[20]
5. State and federal attorney general opinions are available at the respective Department of Justice website.
6. All of these rules are available in browsable and/or searchable form on at least one of the three large commercial databases, Westlaw, Lexis, and Bloomberg.

---

18. usdoj.gov/olc/opinions.

19. For a discussion of how Attorney General Opinions are researched, drafted, and published, see the "Memorandum for Attorneys of the Office, RE: Best Practices for OLC Legal Advice and Written Opinions" at justice.gov/olc/preparation-opinions.html.

20. americanbar.org/products.

Chapter Ten

Legal Citation

I. Introduction

A legal writer's central goal is to convince the reader that the analysis or argument communicated in a document is well-researched and well-supported. To achieve this goal, a legal writer must include references to the authorities used to develop and support the analysis or argument. These references are called *legal citations*, and they serve several critical functions.

- They show the reader **what** authorities support the points made within the document.
- They show the reader **where** to find those authorities.
- They show the reader **who** created those authorities.
- They show the reader **when** the authorities were created.
- They show the reader the **degree of support** those authorities provide.

As a good legal researcher, you should pay attention to citations as you move through the research process. Looking closely at the citations of the authorities you find will help you assess the value of those authorities relative to your research question, and it will help you prioritize your work as you begin to dig deeper into the authorities. For example, if you are working on an issue governed by North Carolina law in a matter that is likely to be filed in a North Carolina state court, you should prioritize cases from North Carolina courts over cases from other states' courts or from federal courts.

You should also make a point of including citations in the research record or log[1] you are creating as you move through the research process. This practice is important for several reasons. First, writing down the citations to the authorities you find *as you find them* will help you avoid unnecessarily retracing

1. See Appendix D for a discussion of strategies for keeping track of your research.

your steps later in your research. Second, it will allow someone familiar with the legal topic (perhaps your professor or your supervisor) to confirm that you searched relevant sources and to determine whether you missed any important sources. Third, it will help future researchers who may use your work on a particular issue as a starting point for their research on the same or a similar issue.

When you write a document for a legal reader, you must give the legal citation for each rule of law and each explanation of the law in the document. By examining the citation for a particular authority, the reader can evaluate the strength of that authority and its usefulness in resolving the issue(s) the document addresses. For example, the reader can determine whether the authority is primary or secondary; whether it is mandatory or persuasive; whether it is older or newer; and whether it supports a proposition directly or only implicitly. Complete and accurate citations also show the reader that your work (and you) can be trusted.

You will find that in law practice, various jurisdictions have their own statutes, court rules, and/or style manuals that dictate the preferred or required form for legal citations. You may find that your employer has its own preference for citation or makes minor variations to generally accepted format. Some law offices have their own style manuals, drawn from state rules and national manuals. Once you are aware of the basic function and format of legal citations, adapting to a slightly different set of rules is not difficult.

This chapter does not attempt to cover the many different legal citation systems that exist among jurisdictions. Rather, it focuses on the most commonly used national citation manual, *The Bluebook: A Uniform System of Citation.*[2] As you will see, North Carolina courts require citations that comport with the current edition of the *Bluebook*.

II. The *Bluebook*

Student editors of four Ivy League law reviews have developed citation rules that are published as *The Bluebook: A Uniform System of Citation*, now in its twentieth edition (published in 2015).[3] For most of the last century, the *Bluebook* was the only national citation system that was widely recognized. Although

---

2. *The Bluebook: A Uniform System of Citation* (Columbia Law Review Ass'n et al. eds., 20th ed. 2015) (hereinafter *Bluebook)*.

3. The twenty-first edition of the *Bluebook* is scheduled to be published in 2020.

law firms, agencies, and organizations consider *Bluebook* citations the norm, many practicing lawyers do not know its current rules; most assume that the *Bluebook* rules have not changed since they were in law school. This is an erroneous and dangerous assumption, and attorneys who take seriously their duty of diligence should habitually check all citations in all documents against the current edition of the *Bluebook.*

For practicing attorneys, the primary difficulty with the *Bluebook* is that it includes *two* citation systems: one for law review articles and another for legal memoranda and court documents. Most of the *Bluebook*'s over 500 pages (the Whitepages) are devoted to citations used for articles published in law reviews and journals. The rules most important to attorneys, those concerning legal memoranda and court documents, are given less attention; they are covered primarily in the Bluepages section of the *Bluebook.* Sections C and D below provide more details about the content of the Whitepages and the Bluepages, respectively.

Fortunately, although the *Bluebook* has become thicker due to the explosion of online sources of legal authority and the growing need to cite international materials, it has also become more user-friendly in some ways. In fact, there is now an online edition of the *Bluebook* available for purchase.[4] Navigating the online *Bluebook* should be fairly easy for attorneys who are comfortable with navigating Westlaw, Lexis, and other commercial platforms.

Below is a brief description of the various sections of the twentieth edition of the *Bluebook.*

A. Quick Reference Guides (inside front and back covers)

Inside the front cover of the *Bluebook* is the "Quick Reference: Law Review Footnotes." This table "gives examples of commonly used citation forms printed in the typefaces used in law review footnotes."[5] It also refers to the relevant rules within the Whitepages (see below) that provide detailed instructions for constructing law review citations to various kinds of legal authorities.

Inside the back cover of the *Bluebook* is the "Quick Reference: Court Documents and Legal Memoranda." This table "gives examples of commonly used citation forms printed in the typefaces used in briefs and legal memoranda."[6] It also refers to the relevant rules within the Bluepages (see below) that provide

4. *See* legalbluebook.com/.
5. *Bluebook,* inside front cover.
6. *Bluebook,* inside back cover.

detailed instructions for constructing citations to various kinds of legal authorities within practitioner documents.

B. Preface, Table of Contents, and Introduction

The Preface to the Twentieth Edition of the *Bluebook* describes the differences between the Twentieth Edition and the Nineteenth Edition. The Preface is short and probably merits a quick read if you are new to the Twentieth Edition. The Table of Contents is actually quite useful; it lists the topic of each *Bluebook* rule and sub-rule, providing a good overview of how the rules are arranged and allowing users to quickly locate the relevant rules for various types of authority.

The Introduction covers basic information about the structure of the *Bluebook* and general principles of citation. The Introduction acknowledges that "[b]ecause of the ever-increasing range of authorities cited in legal writing, no system of citation can be complete."[7] It then suggests that "when citing material of a type not explicitly discussed in this book, try to locate an analogous type of authority that is discussed and use that citation form as a model."[8]

C. Bluepages

The Bluepages (currently pages 3 through 56) were introduced in the eighteenth edition of the *Bluebook*. They provide instructions and examples for constructing citations in documents other than law review articles—most notably, in practitioner documents. The first nine Bluepages rules, B1 through B9, cover information relevant to all types of authority—basic citation structure, typeface for court documents,[9] short citation forms, quotations, abbreviations, numerals, symbols, italicization and capitalization, and titles of judges. Rules B10 through B21 cover citation forms for many of the most commonly cited types of authority, including cases, constitutions, statutes and rules, legislative and administrative materials, books, periodicals, court and litigation documents, Internet sources, and foreign and international materials.

The Bluepages contain two tables. The first table covers suggested abbreviations for words commonly found in the titles of court documents, and the

7. *Bluebook, Introduction*, page 1.

8. *Id.*

9. *See Bluebook* Rule B2, page 7 for a helpful chart comparing the typeface differences between academic citations and non-academic citations.

second table lists jurisdiction-specific court rules and other authorities that govern legal citation.

D. Whitepages

The Whitepages (currently pages 57–231) are "the heart of the *Bluebook* system of citation" according to the authors.[10] There are two main sections within the Whitepages: Rules 1 through 9, which establish "general standards of citation and style for use in all forms of legal writing," and Rules 10 through 21, which "present rules for citation of specific kinds of authority such as cases, statutes, books, periodicals, and foreign and international materials."[11] Although practitioners will rely more heavily on the Bluepages than on the Whitepages, the Bluepages do sometimes reference rules contained in the Whitepages.

E. Tables

The blue-bordered Tables section contains sixteen tables that are used in conjunction with the *Bluebook* rules. *Bluebook* users will see references to these tables throughout both the Bluepages and the Whitepages. Of particular note is Table T1, which contains information about the preferred sources of citation for all United States jurisdictions, both federal and state. The preferred sources of citation for North Carolina cases, statutes, session laws, administrative compilation, and administrative register currently appear on pages 283–84 of Table T1.

F. Index

The Index in the back of the *Bluebook* is quite extensive, and in most instances, it is more helpful than the Table of Contents. Thus, when searching for information about the components of a citation for a specific kind of source, or information about how to format a specific citation, the Index is often your best starting point. Page numbers in black type refer to citation instructions, while page numbers in blue type refer to examples. Remember that the examples in the body of the *Bluebook* are in law review style. When writing a document other than a law review article, you will also need to refer to the practitioners' notes in the Bluepages and the examples inside the back cover to determine whether and how to modify the examples in the Whitepages.

---

10. *Bluebook, Introduction*, page 1.

11. *Id.*

III. North Carolina Citation Rules

The few local citation rules for North Carolina are contained in the North Carolina Rules of Appellate Procedure. Appendix B of those Rules states, "Citations should be made according to the most recent edition of The Bluebook: A Uniform System of Citation."[12] It further states, "Citations to regional reporters shall include parallel citations to official state reporters."[13] Thus, when citing decisions from the North Carolina Supreme Court to courts in North Carolina, the writer must include citations to the official *North Carolina Reports* and the unofficial *South Eastern Reporter* (now in its second series). And when citing decisions from the North Carolina Court of Appeals to courts in North Carolina, the writer must include citations to the official *North Carolina Court of Appeals Reports* and the *South Eastern Reporter.* This parallel citation rule may seem outdated in the age of electronic research, when a case can be pulled up on Westlaw, Lexis, or Bloomberg using either citation; but until the North Carolina Rules of Appellate Procedure change in this regard, the parallel citation rule should be observed.

Even in documents that will not be submitted to a North Carolina court, lawyers practicing in North Carolina often include parallel citations. In such documents, however, it is correct according to the *Bluebook* to cite only to the unofficial *South Eastern Reporter* and then include the abbreviation for the deciding court in the date parenthetical (so the reader will know whether the case is from the Supreme Court or the Court of Appeals).

North Carolina Rule of Appellate Procedure 30(e) governs the use of unpublished opinions issued by North Carolina courts in documents submitted to North Carolina courts. Rule 30(e) provides,

> An unpublished decision of the North Carolina Court of Appeals does not constitute controlling legal authority. Accordingly, citation of unpublished opinions in briefs, memoranda, and oral arguments in the trial and appellate divisions is disfavored, except for the purpose of establishing claim preclusion, issue preclusion, or the law of the case. If a party believes, nevertheless, that an unpublished opinion has precedential value to a material issue in the case and that there is no published opinion that would serve as well, the party may cite the unpublished opinion if that party serves a copy thereof on all other parties in the case and on the court to which the citation is offered. This service may be accomplished by including the copy of the un-

12. N.C. R. App. P. Appendix B.
13. *Id.*

> published opinion in an addendum to a brief or memorandum. A party who cites an unpublished opinion for the first time at a hearing or oral argument must attach a copy of the unpublished opinion relied upon pursuant to the requirements of Rule 28(g). When citing an unpublished opinion, a party must indicate the opinion's unpublished status.[14]

In the context of this rule, "unpublished" means not designated for publication in the official North Carolina reporter. Of course, today there is really no such thing as an "unpublished" opinion, because even cases that are designated "not for publication" by the issuing courts are published on commercial platforms like Westlaw and Lexis. If your research leads you to such a case, consider carefully whether it meets the criteria laid out in Rule 30(e). If you decide it does, and you cite the case in your document, be sure to indicate that the opinion is unpublished and include a copy of the opinion in an appendix to the document.

For attorneys who practice in North Carolina appellate courts, a helpful resource is *A Style Manual for the North Carolina Rules of Appellate Procedure*, published by the Appellate Rules Committee of the North Carolina Bar Association.[15] The Manual represents the Committee's effort to synthesize the Rules and the accompanying appendices into a set of practical examples appellate lawyers can consult. The most recent version of the Manual was published in April 2017, after several amendments to the Rules took effect. According to the Committee, the Manual "is not a substitute for the North Carolina Rules of Appellate Procedure ... and [p]ractitioners are strongly advised to consult the Rules at each stage of the appeal to acquaint themselves with the process, and to read appellate opinions that interpret the Rules."[16]

IV. Other States' Citation Rules

When working in another state, follow that state's local citation rules (Bluepages Table BT2 is a great source of information) or use the format given in the *Bluebook* or another citation manual, depending on your supervisor's preferences. In the state of Washington, for example, the Office of Reporter of Decisions publishes a style sheet that determines citations to be used in doc-

---

14. N.C. R. App. P. 30(e).

15. ncbar.org/media/558476/appellatestylemanual.pdf.

16. Appellate Rules Committee of the N.C. Bar Association, *A Style Manual for the North Carolina Rules of Appellate Procedure* 3 (2017).

uments submitted to Washington courts.[17] The abbreviations required by that style sheet are familiar to lawyers practicing in Washington but may be confusing to lawyers elsewhere.

V. Basic Citation Forms

A. Case Citations

1. Full Case Citations

A full citation to a case includes (1) the name of the case, (2) the volume and reporter in which the case is published, (3) the first page of the case, (4) the exact page in the case that contains the proposition you are citing (i.e., the *pinpoint* or *jump* cite), (5) the court that decided the case, and (6) the date the case was decided.[18] Sometimes you must also include (7) the subsequent history of the case. Below are full citations for a North Carolina Supreme Court case and a North Carolina Court of Appeals case, both with and without parallel citations. These examples are followed by specific information about the various components of a full citation.

- *State v. Walker*, 316 N.C. 33, 37, 340 S.E.2d 80, 87 (1986).
- *State v. Walker*, 340 S.E.2d 80, 87 (N.C. 1986).
- *Mecklenburg Cty. v. Simply Fashion Stores, Ltd.*, 208 N.C. App. 664, 670, 704 S.E.2d 48, 52 (2010).
- *Mecklenburg Cty. v. Simply Fashion Stores, Ltd.*, 704 S.E.2d 48, 52 (N.C. Ct. App. 2010).

a. Case Name

Include the name of only the first party on each side, even if several parties are listed in the case caption. If the party is an individual, include only the party's last name. If the party is a business or organization, shorten the party's name by using abbreviations provided in Table T6 of the *Bluebook*.[19]

Between the parties' names, place a lower case "v" followed by a period. Do not use a capital "V" or the abbreviation "vs." Place a comma after the second party's name, but do not italicize or underline this comma.

---

17. courts.wa.gov/appellate_trial_courts/supreme/?fa=atc_supreme.style.
18. *Bluebook* Rule B10, pages 10–17.
19. *Bluebook* Table T6, pages 496–98.

The parties' names may be italicized or underlined.[20] Use the style preferred by your office, and use that style consistently throughout each document. Do not combine italics and underlining in one cite or within a single document.

b. Volume Number and Reporter

Consult *Bluebook* Table T1 to determine the correct abbreviation for the reporter containing the case you are citing. When including the abbreviation for the reporter in which the case is found, pay special attention to whether the reporter is in its first, second, or third series.[21]

c. Page Numbers

After the reporter name, include the number of the page on which the case begins. Then include the number of the page containing the proposition that you are referencing (the pinpoint page), separated from the initial page number by a comma and a space.[22] If the pinpoint page you are citing is also the first page of the case, then the same page number will appear twice.[23]

d. Deciding Court

In parentheses (separated from the pinpoint page by one space), give the correct abbreviation for the court that decided the case.[24] Table T1 of the *Bluebook* contains the abbreviations for the courts of each jurisdiction. You may also need to consult Tables T7 (Court Names) and T10 (Geographical Terms) to determine the complete abbreviation for the deciding court.

If the reporter abbreviation clearly indicates what court decided a case, do not repeat this information in the parenthetical. For example, only cases of the Supreme Court of the United States are reported in *United States Reports*, abbreviated U.S. Repeating the court notation (U.S.) in the parenthetical of a

---

20. *Bluebook* Rule B2, page 6.

21. The *Bluebook* does not have a comprehensive list of abbreviations for common reporters; consult Table T1 on pages 233–306 for reporter abbreviations for particular U.S. jurisdictions. Abbreviations for reporters for North Carolina cases are located on pages 283–84.

22. *Bluebook* Rule B10.1.2, pages 12–13.

23. When using an online version of a case, remember that a reference to a specific reporter page may change in the middle of a computer screen or a printed page. Thus, the page number indicated at the top of the screen or printed page may not be the page where the relevant information is located. For example, if the notation *821 appears in the text before the relevant information, the pinpoint cite would be to page 821, not page 820.

24. *Bluebook* Rule B10.1.3, page 13.

citation to that reporter would be duplicative. In contrast, *South Eastern Reporter, Second Series*, abbreviated S.E.2d, publishes decisions from different courts within several states, so the abbreviation for the court that decided a particular case must be indicated parenthetically.[25]

Note that the abbreviations for some state courts are not the same as the postal codes for those states. For example, abbreviating the California Supreme Court as either CA or Calif. would be incorrect.

e. Date of Decision

For cases published in reporters, give only the year of decision, not the month or date.[26] Do not include the date on which the case was argued or submitted, the date on which a motion for rehearing was denied, or the publication date of the reporter.[27]

f. Prior and Subsequent History

The *Bluebook* requires that in some instances, the case citation must show what happened to the case at an earlier or later stage of litigation. If the case you are citing was later affirmed or reversed, you must indicate that, as shown in this example:

> *Johnson v. Johnson*, 461 S.E.2d 369, 373 (N.C. Ct. App. 1995), *rev'd*, 468 S.E.2d 59 (N.C. 2006).

Even when you are not required to include the prior or subsequent history of a case, there are instances where you would want to do so, to help the reader understand the weight of the case you are citing. For example:

> The only time that the Supreme Court addressed the requirement of motive for an EMTALA claim, the Court rejected that requirement. *Roberts v. Galen of Va.*, 525 U.S. 249, 253 (1999), *rev'g* 111 F.3d 405 (6th Cir. 1997).

If you are citing a case for a court's analysis of one issue and a later court reversed on a different issue, you need to alert your reader to that, as shown in this example:

---

25. Thus, in the *Mecklenburg Cty.* case, "N.C. Ct. App." indicates that the decision came from the North Carolina Court of Appeals, rather than from another court whose decisions are also published in this reporter.

26. For cases available only online, give the month abbreviation, date, and year. *Bluebook* Rule B10.1.4, page 14.

27. *Bluebook* Rule B4.1.3, page 10 and Rule 10.5, page 106.

Armstrong v. Ledges Homeowners Ass'n, Inc., 620 S.E.2d 294, 300 (N.C. Ct. App. 2005), *rev'd on other grounds*, 633 S.E.2d 78 (N.C. 2006).

If you decide for historical purposes to discuss a case that was later overruled, your reader needs to know that as soon as you introduce the case, as shown in this example:

State v. Melton, 122 S.E. 17, 25 (N.C. 1924), *overruled, State v. Hunt,* 197 S.E.2d 513 (N.C. 1973).

Prior and subsequent history are appended to the full citation, separated by a comma. Abbreviations for the common terms describing prior and subsequent history (*affirming, reversing, overruled,* etc.) are located in Table T8 of the *Bluebook.*[28]

2. Short Case Citations

After a full citation has been used once to introduce an authority, short citations are used for subsequent citations to the same authority. A short citation provides just enough information to allow the reader to locate the longer citation and find the pinpoint page.[29]

When the short cite is to the same source as the immediately preceding citation, use *id.* as the short cite. *Id.* standing alone is sufficient when the short cite is to the same page as the previous citation; but when the short cite is to a different page within the same source, the *id.* must be followed by "at" and the new pinpoint page number. Capitalize *id.* when it begins a citation sentence, just as the first letter of the first word of any sentence is capitalized.[30]

When you are short-citing a case that does not appear in the immediately preceding citation, you cannot use *id.* You must use a short name of one of the parties (generally the first party named in the full cite), the volume, the reporter, and the pinpoint page following "at."[31] For example:

A defendant is not liable for the alienation of affection simply because she has "becom[e] the object of the affections that are alienated from a spouse." *Peake v. Shirley,* 427 S.E.2d 885, 887 (N.C. Ct. App. 1993). There must be "active participation, initiative or encouragement on the part of the defendant in causing one spouse's loss of the other spouse's affections for liability to arise." *Heist v. Heist,* 265 S.E.2d 434,

28. *Bluebook* Table T8, pages 500–01.
29. *Bluebook* Rule B10.2, pages 16–17.
30. *Bluebook* Rule B10.2, page 16.
31. *Bluebook* Rule B10.2, pages 16–17.

> 440 (N.C. Ct. App. 1980). However, it is not necessary that the malicious conduct of the defendant, by itself, provoke the alienation of affections. *Peake*, 427 S.E.2d at 887.

If you refer to the case by name in the sentence, you do not need to repeat the case name in your short citation, though lawyers often do.[32] The last sentence of the example would also be correct as follows:

> *Peake* does not require that the malicious conduct of the defendant, by itself, provoke the alienation of affections. 427 S.E.2d at 887.

When short citing, it is never correct to use only a case name and page number; the volume number and reporter abbreviation are also required.

- Incorrect: *Peake* at 887.
- Correct: *Peake*, 427 S.E.2d at 887.

B. North Carolina Statutory Citations

The official version of the North Carolina General Statutes is published by Lexis.[33] A full citation to a provision in the North Carolina General Statutes includes the title number, code abbreviation, section number, and the date of the hardbound volume in which the current version of the statutory provision is published (not the date it was enacted). If the language you are citing appears only in the pocket part, include only the date of the pocket part.[34] If the language of a portion of the statute is reprinted in the pocket part, include the dates of both the bound volume and the pocket part.[35]

> Example: N.C. Gen. Stat. § 50-13.1 (2017).

C. Federal Statutory Citations

The general rule for citing federal statutes is to cite the *United States Code* (U.S.C.), which is the official code for federal statutes.[36] In reality, that publication is published so slowly that the current language will most likely be found

32. *Bluebook* Rule B10.2, page 16.
33. *Bluebook* Table T1, page 284.
34. *Bluebook* Rule 3.1(c), page 71.
35. *Id.*
36. *Bluebook* Rule B12.1.1, page 18 and Rule 12.2.1, page 121.

in a commercial annotated code, either *United States Code Annotated* (published by West) or *United States Code Service* (currently published by Lexis).

A cite to a federal statute includes the title number, code abbreviation, section number, publisher (except for U.S.C.), and date. As with North Carolina statutory citations, the date given in federal statutory citations is the date of the hardbound volume in which the statute is published, not the date the statute was enacted. If the language you are citing appears only in the pocket part, include only the date of the pocket part.[37] If the language of a portion of the statute is reprinted in the pocket part, include the dates of both the bound volume and the pocket part.[38] For example:

- 14 U.S.C.A. § 736 (West Supp. 2007).
  (Statutory language appears only in the supplemental pocket part.)
- 14 U.S.C.A. § 740 (West 1990 & Supp. 2007).
  (Statutory language appears in both the bound volume and the supplemental pocket part.)

D. Signals

A citation must show the level of support each authority provides. Introductory signals can often be helpful (and are sometimes required) to show this support. The more common signals are explained in Table 10-1.[39]

Table 10-1. Common Signals

No signal	The source cited provides direct support for the idea in the sentence. The citation identifies the source of a quotation.
See	The source cited offers implicit support for the idea in the sentence. The source cited offers support in dicta.
See also	The source cited provides additional support for the idea in the sentence. The support offered by *see also* is not as strong or direct as authorities preceded by no signal or by the signal *see*.
E.g.	Multiple authorities state the idea in the sentence, and you are citing only one as an example; this signal allows you to cite just one source while letting the reader know that other sources say the same thing.

37. *Bluebook* Rule 3.1(c), page 71.
38. *Id.*
39. *Bluebook* Rule B1.2, pages 4–5.

E. Explanatory Parentheticals

An explanatory parenthetical following a citation can convey helpful additional information in a compressed space.[40] Sometimes this parenthetical information conveys to the reader the weight of the authority. For example, a case may have been decided *en banc* or *per curiam*. Or the case may have been decided by a plurality of the judges who heard the case.[41] Parenthetical information also allows you to name the judges who joined in a dissenting, concurring, or plurality opinion.[42] When using this type of parenthetical, be sure that you do not inadvertently hide a critical part of the court's analysis at the end of a long citation, where a reader is likely to skip over it. For example:

> Excluding relevant evidence during a sentencing hearing may deny the criminal defendant due process. *Green v. Georgia*, 442 U.S. 95, 97 (1979) (per curiam) (regarding testimony of co-defendant's confession in rape and murder case).

See Section VI.2 below for more information about using parentheticals effectively.

F. Quotations

Quotations should be used only when the reader needs to see the text exactly as it appears in the original authority. For example, quoting the controlling statutory language can be extremely helpful. As another example, if a well-known case explains an analytical point in a particularly insightful way, a quotation may be warranted.

Excessive quoting has two drawbacks. First, quotations interrupt the flow of your writing when the style of the quoted language differs from your own. Second, excessive quoting may suggest to the reader that you do not fully comprehend the material; it is much easier to cut and paste together a document from pieces of various cases than to synthesize and explain a rule of law. Quotations should not be used simply because you cannot think of another way to express an idea.

When a quotation is needed, the words, punctuation, and capitalization within the quotation marks must appear *exactly* as they are in the original.[43]

---

40. *Bluebook* Rule B1.3, pages 5–6.
41. *Bluebook* Rule B1.3, pages 5–6, and Rule 1.5, pages 64–65.
42. *Id.*
43. *Bluebook*, Rule 5, pages 82–86.

Treat a quotation as a photocopy of the original text. Any alterations or omissions must be indicated. Include commas and periods inside quotation marks; place other punctuation outside the quotation marks unless they are included in the original text. Also, take care to provide smooth transitions between your text and the quoted text.

G. Additional Citation Details

The following citation details are second nature to careful and conscientious lawyers, though they frequently trip up novices.

Use proper ordinal abbreviations. Among the most common errors are using *2nd* instead of *2d* for "Second" and *3rd* instead of *3d* for "Third" because they differ from the standard format.[44]

Do not insert a space between abbreviations of single capital letters. For example, there is no space in the abbreviation "U.S." Ordinal numbers like 1st, 2d, and 3d are considered single capital letters for purposes of this rule. Thus, there is no space in P.2d or F.3d because *2d* and *3d* are considered single capital letters. Leave one space between elements of an abbreviation that are not single capital letters. For example, N.C. Ct. App. has a space on each side of "Ct."[45]

In citation sentences, abbreviate case names, court names, months, and reporter names. Do not abbreviate these words when they are part of textual sentences; instead, spell them out as in the example below.[46]

> The Fourth Circuit held that North Carolina General Statute § 14-208.18(a)(2) was unconstitutional. *Doe v. Cooper*, 842 F.3d 833, 847–48 (4th Cir. 2016).

It is most common in legal documents to spell out numbers zero through ninety-nine and to use numerals for larger numbers. However, always spell out a number that is the first word of a sentence.[47]

H. Citations Not Covered in the *Bluebook*

As comprehensive as the *Bluebook* is, it does not definitively answer every citation question. If you cannot find a specific *Bluebook* rule to cover a source you need to cite, look for rules regarding analogous sources. In creating a ci-

44. *Bluebook* Rule 6.2(b), page 89.
45. *Bluebook* Rule 6.1, pages 87–88.
46. *Bluebook* Rule 10.2, pages 96–102.
47. *Bluebook* Rule 6.2(a), pages 88–89.

tation, always be guided by the purpose of citation: to tell the reader what authority you are citing, who created it, where to find it, and the level and weight of support it provides.

VI. Incorporating Citations into a Document Effectively

A legal document must provide a citation for each statement that comes from a case, statute, article, or other source. Typically, legal citations are included in the text of legal documents rather than in footnotes, end notes, or a bibliography. The *Bluebook* states, "In non-academic legal documents, such as briefs and opinions, citations generally appear within the text of the document immediately following the propositions they support. Footnotes should only be used in non-academic legal documents when permitted or required by local court rules."[48] While you may feel that these in-text citations clutter your documents, most legal readers appreciate being able to see the valuable information the citations provide immediately after reading the points they support.

A citation may offer support for an entire sentence or for an idea expressed in part of a sentence. If the citation supports the entire sentence, it is placed in a separate *citation sentence* that begins with a capital letter and ends with a period.[49] If the citation supports only a portion of the sentence, it is included immediately after the relevant part of that sentence and set off from the sentence by commas in what is called a *citation clause*.[50] Below are examples of each.

- *Citation sentence*: First-degree trespass involves entering or remaining in a building of another without authorization. N.C. Gen. Stat. § 14-159.12 (2018). The term "building" is defined as "any structure or part of a structure, other than a conveyance, enclosed so as to permit reasonable entry only through a door and roofed to protect it from the elements." N.C. Gen. Stat. § 14-159.11 (2018).
- *Citation clause*: North Carolina statutes define both first-degree trespass, N.C. Gen. Stat. § 14-159.12 (2018), and second-degree trespass, N.C. Gen. Stat. § 14-159.13 (2018).

Citations are neither required nor appropriate when you are stating your own conclusions about how a case, statute, or other authority applies to the

48. *Bluebook* Rule B1.1, page 3.
49. *Bluebook* Rule B1.1, page 4.
50. *Id.*

facts of your client's situation. For example, the following sentence should not be followed by a citation: "Under the facts presented, our client's conduct would fall under first-degree burglary because a homeless family sometimes slept in the building he broke into." The facts of your client's case (or research problem in a class assignment) are unique to your situation and would not require a citation. (In a document to a court, however, you may need to cite to the record or to individual filings in the case when citing these facts.) Additionally, conclusions, such as the one above, that are unique to your situation would also not be found in any published source. (In some instances, the use of the signal "*see*" along with a citation to a precedential case that has similar facts may be appropriate.)

While the *Bluebook* is full of specific rules for citing various kinds of legal authority, it does not address many of the "best practices" that have become customary in legal writing. Below are some of these "best practices" that will help you cite more effectively, whether you are in North Carolina or another jurisdiction.

1. Use string citations carefully in briefs and court documents.

A string citation is just what the term suggests: an often lengthy string of citations to authorities that all support a single proposition. Nothing in the *Bluebook* prohibits the use of string citations, but you should use them sparingly; many legal readers would readily admit that they rarely read string citations.

In an effective string citation, each authority is there for a reason. The reader does not benefit from a string citation that serves only to "bulk up" the memo or brief. "Judges and practitioners who read court documents and legal memoranda typically want to see only those authorities that provide the best and strongest support for a stated proposition."[51] For example, string citing several cases from different jurisdictions is useful to the reader when the citations illustrate a trend among federal circuit courts of appeal; but when the proposition you need to support is well-settled in your jurisdiction, one citation to a case from the highest court will likely suffice.

2. Use explanatory parentheticals following your citations if they will help the reader understand the significance of the cited authorities.

An explanatory parenthetical is a device that briefly explains the relationship between a particular authority and the proposition it follows. For example, to

51. ALWD & Colleen M. Barger, *ALWD Guide to Legal Citation* 34.3(a) (6th ed. 2017) (hereinafter *ALWD Guide*).

support a synthesized rule, you must cite two or more cases; this results in a string citation. Inserting an explanatory parenthetical after each citation in the string allows you to show the relevance of each case briefly, without delving into facts and holdings. Here is an example:

> A qualifying expense under the Illinois Family Expense Act includes both household goods and services. *See, e.g.*, *Carter v. Romano*, 662 N.E.2d 883, 884 (Ill. 2007) (doctor and hospital bills); *Armani v. Gucci*, 893 N.E.2d 99, 101 (Ill. App. Ct. 2009) (clothing); *Crocker v. Hines*, 645 N.E.2d 583, 587 (Ill. App. Ct. 1998) (food); *Broyhill v. Lane*, 559 N.E.2d 32, 33 (Ill. App. Ct. 1992) (furniture).[52]

The same caution that applies to string citations applies to explanatory parentheticals: do not overuse them. Professor Richard K. Neumann puts it this way:

> If the material is complicated and important to the issue, explain it in the text. Use an explanatory parenthetical only for information that is simple and not an important part of your discussion or argument. And resist the temptation to use explanatory parentheticals to avoid the hard work of explaining complicated and important authority.[53]

For a fairly straightforward discussion of the practitioner rules governing explanatory parentheticals, see Bluepages Rule B1.3 in the Twentieth Edition of the *Bluebook*.

3. Avoid citation clauses and embedded citations if possible.

As explained above, a citation clause results when a citation supports only part of textual sentence and thus is located within the textual sentence. The *Bluebook* permits citation clauses; in fact, it seems to require them in sentences that contain two propositions that are supported by different authorities.

An embedded citation is also located within the textual sentence and is used to provide the remainder of the citation when the authority itself is named in the textual sentence. For example:

> In *Foster v. Winston-Salem Joint Venture*, 281 S.E.2d 36, 42 (N.C. 1981), the court held that a landowner may be liable for injuries sustained

---

52. *Id.* at 328.

53. Richard K. Neumann, Jr., *Legal Reasoning and Legal Writing: Structure, Strategy, and Style* § 20.4, 266 (5th ed., Aspen Publishers 2005).

by business invitees which are the result of intentional criminal acts of third persons.

Citation clauses and embedded citations present two challenges for the reader. First, they produce unwieldy sentences—sentences that are too long, too choppy, or both. Second, they interrupt the reader's train of thought as he or she tries to understand and absorb the propositions in your sentences. You can almost always avoid citation clauses if you follow the general rule of including only one proposition per sentence—a rule that usually enhances both readability and comprehension. An embedded citation should only be used when the authority itself is part and parcel of the proposition.

VII. *ALWD Guide to Legal Citation*

In 2000, the Association of Legal Writing Directors published the first edition of the *ALWD Citation Manual* as an alternative to the *Bluebook*. Now in its sixth edition, the publication has a new title, the *ALWD Guide to Legal Citation*. The *ALWD Guide* does not create a completely new system of citation; in fact, for all documents, the *ALWD Guide*'s rules are the same as the *Bluebook*'s rules. The chief difference is that the *ALWD Guide* uses just one set of rules for both practitioner documents and law review articles, rather than two separate sets of rules. For practitioner documents, the citations that result from using the *ALWD Guide* are usually identical to those that would result from using the Bluepages of the *Bluebook*.

Although the North Carolina Rules of Appellate Procedure mandate that practitioners in North Carolina cite according to the *Bluebook*, the *ALWD Guide* is nonetheless a very helpful book. It is much more user-friendly than the *Bluebook*, its explanations of citation rules are clear, and its examples are useful to both law students and practicing attorneys. The website of the Association of Legal Writing Directors has detailed information about the *ALWD Guide*, including a correlation chart listing the rules in the sixth edition of the *ALWD Guide* and the corresponding rules in the twentieth edition of the *Bluebook*.[54]

54. alwd.org/wp-content/uploads/2017/09/ALWD_to_BB_6e_correlations.pdf.

VIII. Tools for the Toolbox

1. As you are researching, write down the citations for the sources you find, so you will not have to retrace your steps later when you need to cite to those sources in your document.
2. When writing documents that will be submitted to North Carolina courts, cite your authorities according to the most recent edition of the *Bluebook*, as mandated by Appendix B of the North Carolina Rules of Appellate Procedure.
3. Focus on the Bluepages section of the *Bluebook* when you are constructing citations in practitioner documents.
4. Place citations in the text of your documents, not in footnotes, and avoid strong citations, citation clauses, and embedded citations when possible.

Appendix A

How a Bill Is Enacted into Law in the United States Congress

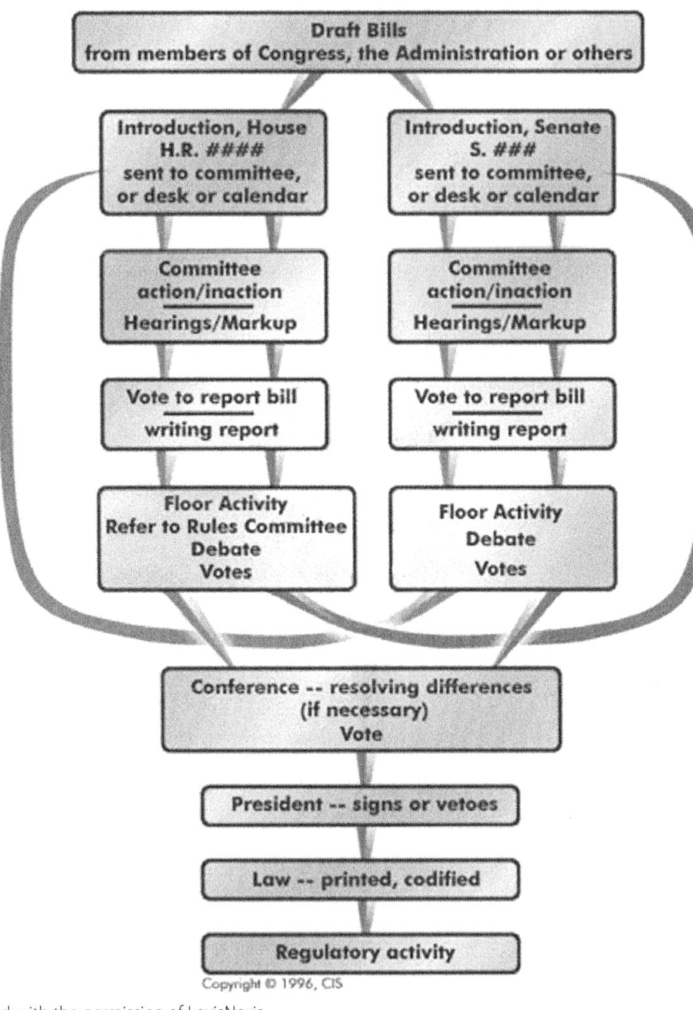

Reprinted with the permission of LexisNexis.

Appendix B

How a Bill Is Enacted into Law in the North Carolina General Assembly

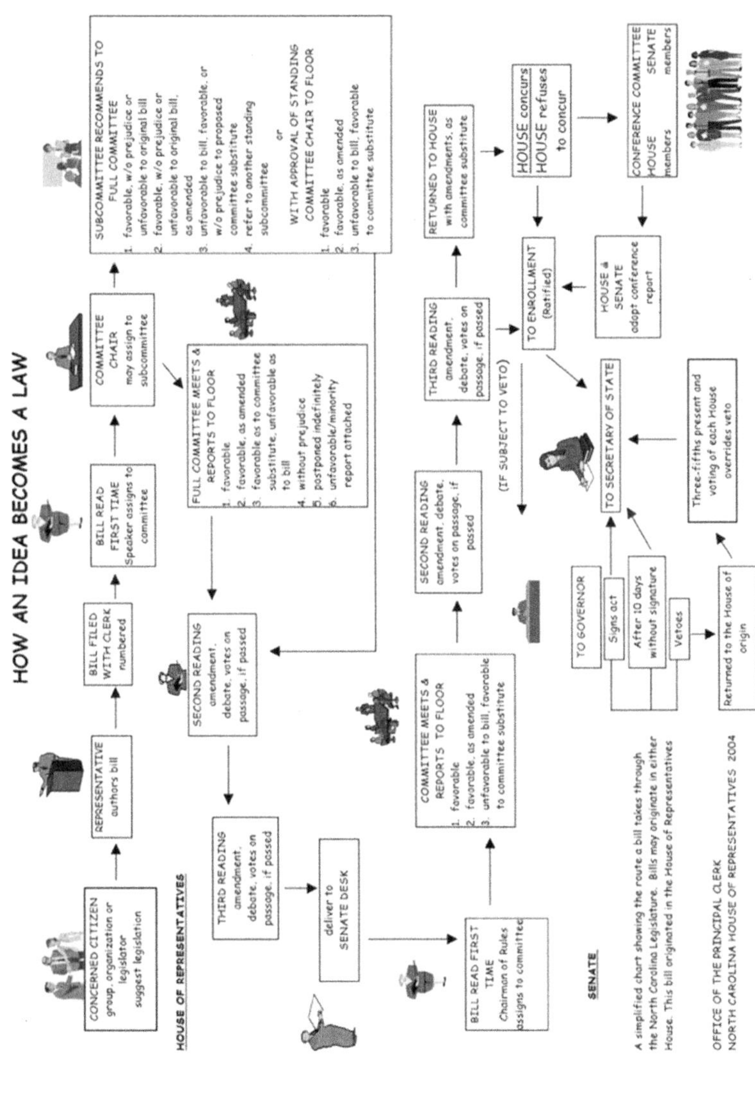

Source: www.ncleg.gov/Content/Documents/HowAnIdeaBecomesALaw.pdf

Appendix C

Geographic Boundaries of United States Courts of Appeals and United States District Courts

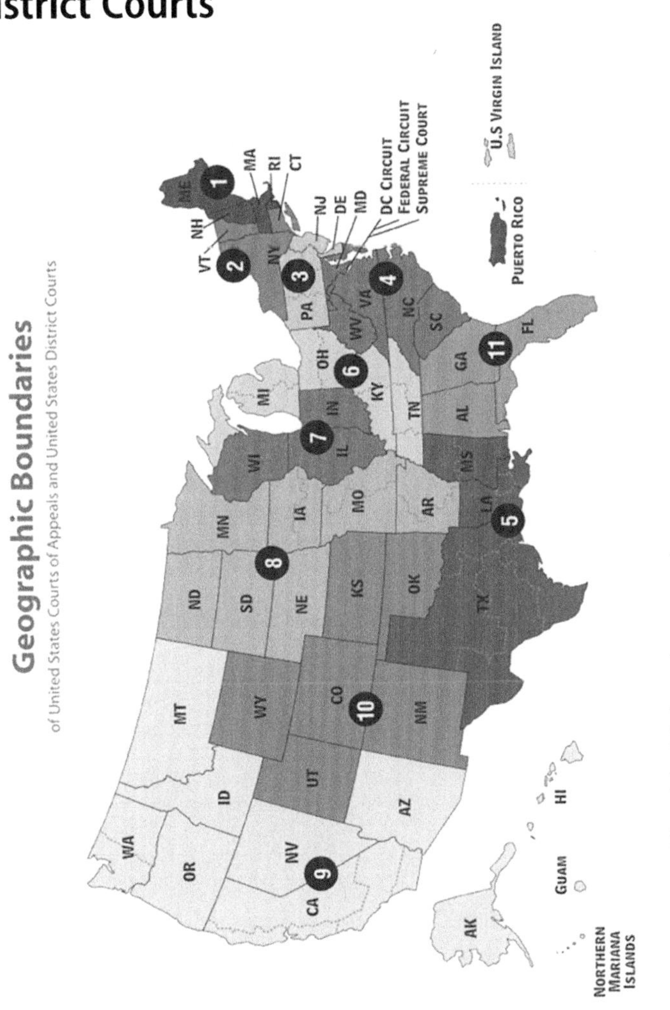

Source: Administrative Office of the U.S. Courts. (uscourts.gov).

Appendix D

Research Log

Research Log For: ____________________

Initial Facts: *Parties, dates, place/jurisdiction, potential causes of action, relief, damages, penalties?*

Client's Goals: *Legal? Non-Legal? Limitations with respect to time spent or resources?*

Research Plan: *Potential sources? How much time? Search terms? Additional information needed?*

Sources Relied Upon — Binding Precedent: *Statutes, Regulations, local law, court rules, cases, administrative decisions (if precedential).*

Sources Consulted — Secondary: *Overview of law; leads to primary law; check multiple research platforms & sources if available; always update & do own analysis of primary law.*

Other Sources — Persuasive Precedent: *If needed or used for research, decisions of lower courts in jurisdiction or other decisions outside jurisdiction.*

Wrap-up: *List KeyCite/Shepard's results for all authority relied upon. Can you fully answer research question? Do you need more information? What remedies/penalties/causes of action are available?*

Abbreviated Checklist* (Use with Research Log)

- Initial Facts
  - Be sure you understand the question you are researching, your client's goals and that you answer ***all*** elements.
  - Note any additional facts that you need. If there are facts you can find through general research, do that research.
  - Dates: be cognizant of your time frame.
  - Think about jurisdiction and the potential for overlapping authority.
- Secondary Sources
  - Use secondary sources as a tool for finding and understanding the primary law. ***ALWAYS*** verify the secondary source's analysis of that primary law by examining it yourself and discussing it with an eye to your client's facts and needs.
  - Remember that different platforms offer different sources, so check elsewhere if you're not finding something useful.
- **Primary Binding Authority**
  - Look for all potentially relevant primary authority. Think about:
    - Potential for overlapping jurisdictions.
    - Potential for multiple relevant sources of primary law (cases, statutes, etc.).
    - Potential for multiple causes of action.
    - ***Don't assume you're done with the first thing you found!***
    - Think about your facts in relation to the primary law e.g., relevant standards, burdens, penalties, remedies, procedural considerations, etc.
  - Statutes and regulations mean what courts/ agencies say they mean; look for ***interpretive*** case law.
- Primary Persuasive Authority
  - Use cases from other jurisdictions for research by looking for binding cases with the same applicable topic & key numbers.
  - Don't cite to persuasive authority if there is mandatory authority on point. Cite to the mandatory authority.
- Wrap-Up
  - Always update primary authority relied upon. If an update is relevant to your client, explain why and when it will be effective.
  - In your research log note any negative treatment and why you can still rely upon the authority.
  - For statutes and regulations, note currency of database and update as necessary to the present day.
  - If pending legislation doesn't impact your facts, note this and move on.

* For more tips, consult the *Student Guide to Superior Legal Research*.

About the Authors

Brenda D. Gibson is Senior Legal Writing Professor and Director of Legal Writing at North Carolina Central University School of Law.

Julie L. Kimbrough is a Clinical Assistant Professor of Law and Deputy Director of the Kathrine R. Everett Law Library at University of North Carolina School of Law.

Laura P. Graham is a Professor of Legal Writing and Director of the Legal Analysis, Writing, and Research Program at Wake Forest University School of Law.

Nichelle J. Perry is an Assistant Professor of Law and the Law Library Director at North Carolina Central University School of Law.

Index